IMPACT MY LIFE

biblical mentoring simplified

Elisa Pulliam

www.moretobe.com

COPYRIGHT

Cover image designed by Elisa Pulliam using image from istock.com and font from Jellyka Nerevan.

dedication

Titus 2:3-5

teach the older women

train the younger women

For this generation of young women desperately longing for older women to speak truth, grace, love, wisdom and hope into their souls as they do life together.

And for especially for my children.

Table of Contents

PREFACE

Live a Life of Impact

> Would you like to gain the skills and confidence to impact the lives of those around you with godly wisdom and relevant Truth?
>
> Have you witnessed the influence of the culture on this generation of young people and would like to be equipped to practically guide them in a biblical direction?
>
> Are you a mom longing to engage with your maturing daughter in a way that is both positive and life transforming?
>
> Have you been approached by a younger woman seeking to be mentored in her faith or life skills, but feel overwhelmed by her request?

Impact My Life offers a true blend of biblical principles, relevant illustrations, life coaching techniques and creative ideas for simplifying mentoring and thereby cultivating influential and healthy relationships that honor God.

The Challenge

As a fellow sojourner on this intentional faith walk, I know the challenges we face as women to feel effective and instrumental in the lives of others. It is all too easy to focus on our weaknesses, while making a myriad of excuses that keep us from being used by God for

His glory in the important relationships that abound in our lives.

For those of us who were not raised with biblical truths and never experienced the benefits of mentoring, it is easy to believe that we could never step into significant mentoring roles. However, I am here to challenge you to think differently about your purpose and potential as a biblical mentor so that you may feel called, qualified and equipped!

Impact My Life will enable you to see yourself being used by the Lord, right here, right now, for the benefit of those people perfectly placed in your corner of the world. Within these pages, you will learn simple and practical ideas for becoming an effective biblical mentor to your own daughters or nieces, a group of teen girls from church or freshman girls in your dorm, a group of young moms or a Bible study for new Christians, a women's ministry leadership team or group of youth leaders, and even your sweet neighbor or colleague who is looking for some wisdom and encouragement.

I can testify from my own lifelong mentoring journey, which has been rewarding and stretching, that our qualifications come from the Lord. He is more than eager to use an enthusiastic soul than a seemingly qualified one. It is the willing spirit that matters, not life experience, a gifted personality or a seemingly perfect life. Expertise and degree qualifications do not matter to hurting hearts, lost souls or women hungry for love wrapped in truth.

The Training

Impact My Life is designed to help you discover your identity as a disciple of Christ and uncover the beauty of being equipped by Him to impact others for His glory. Through a close look at the Scriptures, you'll learn that to mentor biblically you must first follow Christ distinctly. From the overflow of your faith, you will be able to confidently dive into individual mentoring relationships and use the group mentoring format used for hosting and leading Evening Tea & Chat (known as ETC), Mugs & Mornings, and Grace Chats, which I'm excited to share with you in detail throughout later chapters.

Impact My Life is a biblical training manual and a personal devotional study combined! The original content was formed in a 31 Days of Mentoring Training series at *More to Be* and later bound in an eBook by the same title. In this book, however, you will find those powerful truths expanded upon with new personal stories, relevant examples, biblical and life coaching principles, and practical application ideas.

I highly encourage you to invest your heart and mind in the experience of reading *Impact My Life* by taking the time to answer the **Take Time to Train** questions. With a Bible and journal on hand, I recommend devoting fifteen minutes a day to this time of study by recording your answers, reflections and prayers as you move through the material. This dedication of your time will reap dividends as you launch forward into significant mentoring relationships.

I also recommend using *Impact My Life* as a small group study for a women's ministry team, a group of mothers of tween or teenage daughters, or as a short one month study with women interested in launching an mentoring ministry with you. At the end of the book, you will find a Small Group Leader's Guide with suggestions on how to prepare for and lead a small group through this study.

The Impact

You are needed to spread the Good News and the love of Christ with others. God may be calling you to influence a teen directly, your own child, a young mother, or a peer with relevant, biblical truth and the hope of Christ. Regardless of who you may have the opportunity to influence, *Impact My Life* will inspire you to step out in faith, equipped with the Truth, to impact the lives around you.

~ • ~

PART ONE

Simplifying Biblical Mentoring

We're not here for adoration and worship of God only, although that's number one. If that were all we're for, God could take us straight to heaven, where our worship would be undistracted. No, the reason He leaves us here a while is so that we can make a mark on others before we go.

Anne Ortlund
The Gentle Ways of a Beautiful Woman

CHAPTER ONE

It Begins With A Story

I always had a heart for encouraging younger girls and sharing lessons of life with them. Even as far back as high school, I would take a few younger friends under my wing. Once I became a Christian in college, and returned home, I settled into my church and began work with the youth ministry. Two years later, my husband and I began living and working at a boarding school. Living in a dorm with 40 teenage boys from around the world made me pretty desperate for girls of any age, so I slipped over to one of the girls dorm one night a week to "officially" supervise study hours while seizing opportunities to informally mentor.

It was amazing to see how God took the heart I always wore on my sleeve and began using it to minister to these curious young women. Some of them came from broken homes and reckless relationships, full of fear about their futures. Others came from well-caring families, but had real concerns about what life would be like in college and beyond.

As a newly married twenty-something, I had a bit of credibility in their eyes, so they naturally sought my advice. I used these times of answering their questions to also share my testimony. By giving them a piece of my life and sneaking in truths from my spiritual journey, God opened the doors to their heart as I shared vulnerable real life experiences and relevant truth. My life was telling a story about Christ, and the stories written on my heart were revealing the ways of God and His purposes, not only for me, but also for them. In the same way Jesus uses parables in the Scriptures to illustrate God's instructions, my life stories painted a picture of how God works and transforms and makes new all things, offering them hope for their futures and often a new perspective on life.

> *2 Corinthians 3:3*
> *Clearly, you are a letter from Christ showing the result of our ministry among you. This "letter" is written not with pen and ink, but with the Spirit of the living God. It is carved not on tablets of stone, but on human hearts.*

Over the years, my testimony has often been the launching point of my mentoring relationships, however, it doesn't begin and end there. As I walk with the Lord, my life testimony becomes greater than my salvation story. Each lesson learned is a lesson to share. Each act of God's grace is an act to proclaim. Each moment of sin overcome by repentance is one to brag on God about.

Stories set the backdrop for mentoring relationships, offering a personal side considering a biblical truth, which cultivates authentic relationships and a places for teachable moments. It is a natural process that marks sharing life together. All it takes is being willing to expose God's extravagant grace, forgiveness, power to heal, provision and love for the sake of building others up in the faith and pointing them toward Jesus.

These times of storytelling play out when I am sitting on my couch with a teenage girl, listening carefully to her words revealing a hidden heart. I respond with a warm smile, understanding nod and, if appropriate, a lesson learned when I was in her shoes. Depending on her circumstances, that lesson may be similar to one of my own present day struggles. As Solomon declares,

> *Ecclesiastes 1:9*
> *History merely repeats itself. It has all been done before. Nothing under the sun is truly new.*

These stories fold into everyday life and become as much a part of my mentoring as they are a part of my parenting. Real life offers the potential to illustrate biblical principles in ways that a sermon or study alone cannot accomplish. I use stories to draw my children and mentorees into the Scriptures, translating parables into modern day applications. Often, my ETC gatherings begin with a prayed up, thought through, Holy Spirit led story relevant to the topic. It is amazing to watch the Lord use my fumbles and foibles to touch the hearts of a dozen or so teenage girls filling my living room. Their curious minds are hungry for truth, but the pathway to their mind comes through story. They want to be taught, but not lectured. So I share an experience. I reveal a struggle. I confess a lesson learned. I allude to a sin, without the gory details, but to get their attention. From each story, I stroll into the Truth, tying the lesson together with a biblical principle and verses to support the application.

The way we mentor will be entirely unique to the stories we tell. They come from the lessons we've learned, the lives we've lived, and the Christ we love. When used for the glory of God and His purposes, our stories are a powerful tool in impacting others with an eternal perspective.

Take Time to Train

1. Thinking back over your lifetime, can you see evidence of having a heart for younger people? If so, jot down a few words about how that played out in your life.
2. If your heart hasn't necessarily been for younger people, who do you find yourself drawn to? Is there a way God might be leading you to intentionally engage with them as a mentor?
3. What inspires you to want to invest a portion of yourself in others?
4. What is your life story, and in particular your faith journey? Think about this for a moment and see if you can summarize it in a short paragraph. If you have the time, write out your whole story for your own legacy of faith to be recorded.
5. What is a recent story of God at work in your life?

~ • ~

CHAPTER TWO

First Things First

Biblical mentoring is a combination of mentoring and discipleship. Jesus set the example for us in the way He came alongside the disciples, modeled his Father's instructions in action, answered their questions, responded to their needs and challenged them forward in their calling to glorify God. He was both their friend and their teacher. A mentor and a man who discipled others. He set a pattern for us to follow as we answer the call to go forth and make disciples.

> *Matthew 28:19*
> *Therefore go and make disciples of all nations, baptizing them in the name of the Father and of the Son and of the Holy Spirit.*

Discipleship

Although discipleship is commonly referenced and encouraged in Christian communities, it is not restricted to that context. The broad definition of disciple means to be a student of a particular teacher and follower of their doctrine. Within the Christian context, however, that teacher must be Jesus with Scripture as the doctrine. This means that a biblical mentor would agree to these principles:

Principles for Biblical Mentoring

- I engage in an active, personal relationship with Jesus Christ, believing that He died on the cross for the forgiveness of my sins (Romans 10:9-10).

- I seek to learn the Word, apply it to life and follow the leading of the Holy Spirit (Hebrews 4:12, 2 Timothy 3:16).

- I demonstrate an active commitment to the body of Christ by attending church, serving using my gifts and talents, and coming under the authority of a pastor and elders (Romans 12).

If you can agree to each of these statements, you are living as a disciple of Christ, and the overflow of your relationship with Him will purposefully influence others as you lead, teach, model and encourage those you mentor. However, if you are unsure what it means to live as a disciple of Christ in a personal relationship with Jesus as your Savior, I would recommend taking the time now to read the resource tucked in at the end of this book, Beginning as a Disciple of Christ.

Mentoring

Traditionally, mentoring takes place in the workplace or an academic environment, where a seasoned employee or older student comes alongside a younger cohort and trains, guides and encourages that person in a particular area of expertise. Biblical mentoring combines the heart of discipleship and methods of mentoring to cultivate relationships steeped in Truth through living out biblical application side-by-side.

In a biblical mentoring relationship, the goal is to train the younger person or believer in every area of life, not only through teaching but also by example, incorporating God and His word into every teachable spoken and silent moment. This principle is laid out in Deuteronomy 6:5-7, which indicates how to live a life that teaches by example and intentionality, particularly with one's children, but certainly not limited to that relationship.

> *Deuteronomy 6:5-7*
> *And you must love the Lord your God with all your heart, all your soul, and all your strength. And you must commit yourselves wholeheartedly to these commands that I am giving you today. Repeat them again and again to your children. Talk about them when you are at home and when you are on the road, when you are going to bed and when you are getting up.*

In other words, biblical mentoring applies the idea of training up, but expands it beyond the family unit. In a world of divorce and death, children needing mothers and fathers abound. There are an endless number of young people (and young is always relative) without an emotionally or physically present parental unit, desperately needing the practical gift of time, love and personal investment. Using a biblical mentoring approach for how to do life together, brings those lost ones into the fold, offering them life skills and Scripture lived out.

A Titus 2 Focus

As we focus on this idea of biblical mentoring, we'll be honing in on the responsibility of women to train up the next generation. This call is shaped through the Scriptures found in Titus 2:3-5. Paul's instructions to Titus presents a simple but necessary set of expectations on the responsibility of older women:

> *Titus 2:3-5*
> *Similarly, teach the older women to live in a way that honors God. They must not slander others or be heavy drinkers. Instead, they should teach others what is good. These older women must train the younger women to love their husbands and their children, to live wisely and be pure, to work in their homes, to do good, and to be submissive to their husbands. Then they will not bring shame on the word of God.*

Regardless of your age or season of life, this passage from Titus 2 likely applies to you in some manner. Consider if this is where you find yourself:

- Do you find yourself longing for an older woman to speak into your life, but don't know what to do with those feelings?
- Are you the older woman, struggling with feeling out of touch but seeing young women floundering all around you?
- Maybe you're a mom with tween or teenage daughters and you'd like to spend some intentional time training them up, but feel at a loss for where to begin?
- Has the Lord laid it on your heart to start an ETC group, but the whole idea of mentoring is intimidating?

Either you identify with the responsibilities of the older woman in the Titus 2 passage or you long for that woman to step into your life. In the next chapters, I promise to offer you step-by-step instructions and endless words of encouragement for seeing the Titus 2 principle manifest itself in your life, regardless of whether you are looking to be mentored or mentor others.

My desire is to help you see how living as a disciple of Christ, and implementing biblical mentoring principles, will enable you to move out from your excuses and into confidence that God has equipped you for the call to impact the lives of those around you. I also hope you will discover that He is already meeting the need in your life to be mentored, and it is simply a matter of you seeing Him at work in this way.

Take Time to Train

1. Were you able to agree with the Principles for Biblical Mentoring statements? If not, which ones do you struggle with? Would you be willing to speak to a pastor or Christian friend about these concerns?
2. Who has been a biblical mentor to you? How did you learn from them? Be specific as you consider their teaching, example, and encouragement.
3. Who might you be unintentionally discipling or mentoring in your life currently?
4. Is the example you are setting consistent with Scripture and the model Jesus set forth? Take time to explain this answer.
5. Spend ten minutes in quiet prayer, asking Jesus to speak to you directly about your influence on others and, moreover, who you're being influenced by. Make sure you have a Bible on hand and, if you feel the prompting, take the time to read a particular verse or passage. Let the Word change your thinking and transform your life.

~ • ~

CHAPTER THREE

iMentor Manifesto

Let's just put it out there: the term "mentoring" can carry quite a stigma. If a group of women were polled to ask what they think of mentoring, especially within the Christian community, I suspect eight out of ten women would feel "less than" in answering the call to mentor. I'd also guess that many would sheepishly admit they have forever longed to be intentionally mentored by an older, wiser, loving, prayer warrior.

The fact is that many women lack eyes to see the opportunity to mentor and miss noticing when they have been mentored by others. I'd like to challenge you to see mentoring through a whole new perspective. As you read these statements, which I like to call the iMentor Manifesto, I encourage you to consider how many apply to what you are currently experiencing in your life or what you desire to experience in the future.

I Mentor...

- I mentor because I long to see people live according to God's Word, by the power of His strength and in the comfort of His love and grace.
- I mentor because I hope to see God's purpose and potential realized in the life of another woman, regardless of her age.
- I mentor my children through encouraging them in Godly

principles and modeling for them biblical priorities.
- I mentor my spiritual daughter by meeting her practical needs and simply being available to love her as a surrogate mother.
- I mentor women in the body of Christ through teaching those younger in the Word even if they are older in years.
- I mentor younger moms in sharing the lessons learned along my journey of motherhood and encourage them to press into Jesus for their strength.
- I mentor teen girls by devoting time to listen to their stories as I also seek Spirit-appointed opportunities to teach the Truth!
- I mentor others because I love Jesus!
- I mentor because of what Christ has done in my life.

I Am Mentored...

It takes an equally intentional look to recognize the many ways we are mentored by others:
- I am mentored through attending a weekly bible study and experiencing the biblical wisdom and perspective of my small group leader.
- I am mentored through impromptu discussions with my mother-in-law about biblical truth, especially God's sovereignty.
- I am mentored in unexpected Facebook chats with older, Christian friends, checking in on my heart and life and children and family.
- I am mentored by a woman after God's own heart, who simply enjoys time with me sharing a lunch on the porch.
- I am mentored in short little conversations with older women hovering outside the sanctuary after church -- conversations where truth is sown into my soul with a few words of wisdom.
- I am mentored by my dear, dear friends, who are steeped in Scripture and are willing to hold me accountable to living out God's purposes for my life.
- I am mentored through books and studies written by Christian women (and men), as these authors share their faith, life experience and understanding of the Word in a relevant way.

- I am mentored by Christian women who share their hearts, hopes, and the Scriptures through their blog posts (and even in their social media updates), as they challenge my focus and redirect me back to the Lord.
- I am mentored through the Scriptures as I study the Word and submit myself to the guidance of the Holy Spirit.

These mentoring moments may not seem glamorous, but they are incredibly important life-giving conversations, experiences, relationships and circumstances in which God lays before me an example of the Word in action to pattern my life after.

The times of mentoring happen all around me, to me and for me. They are happening around you, to you and for you, too! For many years I missed the reality of mentoring in my life, because I was looking for something more formal with a particular title. It is only when God refined my vision about mentoring that I was I able to receive mentoring moments from others with an open, humble, and grateful heart, and recognize when I might be able to do the same for others.

Take Time to Train

1. How do these mentoring statements challenge you to think differently about the role of a mentor?
2. Which of the statements reflect how you are currently mentoring others or being mentored?
3. Which of the statements would you like to be true for your life today, and what needs to happen in order for that to be the case?
4. Take some time to journal about your thoughts and seek the Lord in prayer in light of thinking differently about mentoring.

~ • ~

CHAPTER FOUR

Qualified by Christ

Most women believe they are not qualified to be a mentor. This is not the truth! If you love Jesus and strive to live according to the Scriptures, then you are qualified to mentor.
We are qualified to mentor biblically when we follow Christ distinctly.

It is time for you to think of mentoring in terms of being a trusted counselor, guide or advocate. In Christ, you are more than qualified to do just that because the Holy Spirit is the one guiding you!

> *John 14:26*
> *But when the Father sends the Advocate as my representative—that is, the Holy Spirit—he will teach you everything and will remind you of everything I have told you.*

Author and speaker, Anne Ortlund writes in *Disciplines of a Beautiful Woman*, that we simply need to know "one more thing" to teach that "one thing" to someone else. For example, once we learn a verse, we can turn to another person and teach that verse. It may be only one verse, but from there we go back to our Bible and learn another verse, so that we can teach again and again.

Mentoring is for Moms

The setting of motherhood makes the biblical mentoring process an absolutely natural experience. As a mom lives out her faith immersed in the Word, she can naturally teach her children through the lens of Biblical truth. In essence, when she thinks of herself as a mentor of her own children, a mom will likely take on the "training up" responsibility with greater discipline and dedication. This need to feed her children spiritual food will motivate her to invest in her own spiritual development and disciplines. It is impossible to teach what we do not know!

Of course, making time for the Lord and the Word requires creativity and accountability. There is no blueprint for how a mom ought to structure her day or her quiet time. Sure, it would be wonderful to be up before the early risers, but that's not always been possible. If you are a mom, especially of little ones, let me encourage you to not let the pressure of your responsibilities deter you from your time with Jesus! I've been known to leave dishes in the sink and pop in a Christian video for the kids, to get with Jesus in the early part of the day. The chores can wait, while you run to spend twenty minutes alone with the Lord.

If you are a busy mom longing for accountability and encouragement from other women, I highly recommend checking out your local church for a women's Bible Study group that offers childcare or a chapter of a Moms in Prayer or MOPS group. Regardless of the age of your children or work situation, you can make the most of online accountability groups, such as Good Morning Girls or Hello Mornings. The fellowship of sisters in Christ will spur you on to investment your time in meeting with the Lord daily and studying His Word. You'll soon find out that the rewards are great, as only a mom growing in her faith through time with Jesus and in the Word will be able to pour new truths upon her children and those she longs to mentor.

Mentoring is for MORE than Moms

Mentoring isn't reserved exclusively for motherhood. If biblical mentoring is simply coming alongside another and offering wisdom, training, commitment and encouragement, then this process can happen within the context of many different types of relationships, such as:

- aunts and nieces
- a college senior and a freshman from her dorm or team
- a high school senior and an elementary school neighbor
- an older woman and a younger woman at church
- a young, spiritually mature woman and even a slightly older new Christian
- a partnership of women hosting a gathering of teens, such as ETC

An older woman might come alongside a young mom at church, even with a simple word for her immediate circumstance. A college girl can mentor a roommate or classmate, helping her to discover her God-given identity and purpose. An older sibling can mentor a young one through reading Scripture together and then talking about how it applies to life. The possibilities of mentoring are endless!

Qualified and Called

Essentially, there are two qualifications for being a biblical mentor:

1. Being committed to the Word as Truth and seeking to live it out daily (2 Timothy 3:16-17).
2. Being open to God's leading in revealing which people in your life are in need of biblical mentoring (Titus 2:3-5).

Biblical mentoring is about doing real life together with real people. It is about being rooted in the Word in order to apply it to everyday life. You are defined as mentor by how you live, day in and day out as a disciple of Christ in relationships with others. It isn't so much about how you mentor, where you mentor, or who you mentor. You don't need a title or program! All you need is to feel the call personally and respond practically.

So, will you consider yourself a biblical mentor from this point forward?

Take Time to Train

1. Do you feel qualified in Christ to mentor? Explain your answer.
2. What is your greatest fear about mentoring?
3. Look up 2 Timothy 3:16-17. How does this change your thinking or encourage you?
4. Are you comfortable with doing real life with others? Why or why not?
5. If you are a mom, how are you doing in your spiritual growth and development? Would it be helpful for you to find an accountability group, such as the ones recommended in this chapter?
6. Prayer is such an essential component of the mentoring journey. Spend five minutes today in prayer for all that the Lord is revealing to you through this study and for His direction in your life.

~ • ~

PART TWO

Eliminating Excuses

Whatever the degree of involvement and however the relationship works itself out, the command is clear. Older women are to encourage and equip younger women to live for God's glory.

Susan Hunt
Spiritual Mothering: The Titus 2 Model for Women Mentoring Women

CHAPTER FIVE

What Did He Say?

Most women can come up with at least one excuse why they can't mentor. Most of their excuses, however, are not rooted in the Truth. The Father of Lies doesn't have to work very hard to get into a woman's secret thoughts and render her utterly insecure about mentoring.

> *John 8:44*
> *...the devil..He was a murderer from the beginning. He has always hated the truth, because there is no truth in him. When he lies, it is consistent with his character; for he is a liar and the father of lies.*

The enemy simply looks at our lives, notes our weakness and fears, and offers up an excuse filled with half truth, half lie. This is exactly what the serpent did in the Garden of Eden when he asked Eve, "Did God really say...?" (Genesis 3:1).

So many times, we're caught in the same cycle of doubting God's plans and purposes for us, and we believe the enemy's accusations and false promises. What begins with an innocent question of doubt opens the door to the deception. The enemy's purpose is clear, every time, as he sets out to steal, kill and destroy us and our influence in this world.

> *John 10:10*
> *The thief's purpose is to steal and kill and destroy. My purpose is to give them a rich and satisfying life.*

When the Devil knocks us out of the game of life, he wipes out all the people God intended for our faith to touch. He eliminates the fullness of God's purpose for us and those we are designed to impact. This is a foundational biblical principle for any disciple of Christ, in any and all circumstances, and it is most certainly true for biblical mentoring.

It is time to tackle these excuses birthed in the labyrinth of lies by looking at truth-filled biblical responses. Are you willing to embark on this investigative journey, laying down your excuses, and discovering truth that will transform your life? I hope so.

Take Time to Train

1. What is your main excuse for not mentoring? Take time to journal about this and seek the Lord in prayer in preparation for our further study about excuses.
2. Do you detect a pattern of thinking in your excuse(s)? If so, explain and look for the root of that particular issue.
3. Have you ever spent time studying about core values and recognizing your beliefs about God, this world, and even yourself? Take time to download Mental Makeover for further study in this area.

~ • ~

CHAPTER SIX

But I'd Be a Hypocrite!

It is natural to resist mentoring as a result of feeling like a hypocrite. Many women would rather slink into the fringes of their faith than step up to guide a younger woman in biblical truth. Past circumstances, in which foolish choices reveal a legacy of shame, prevent many women from instructing their daughters or other women in the body of Christ. They get caught in the false belief of "If I tell her what I did, then she might take that as permission to make the same mistake."

There is wisdom in carefully considering how much information about the past you ought to relay for the purpose of teaching and encouraging. Generalizations are definitely better than details. But stories are a powerful way to illustrate truth. Jesus used stories to teach, presenting parables representing biblical truth. While our stories are not parables, carefully selected portions of our lives can be used to put shape to biblical instructions, demonstrate consequences of sin, and give God the glory for the redemption offered by His grace.

Fear of being exposed or judged also can keep a woman from sharing her experiences and offering valuable life lessons to the next generation. This fear should be a red flag to reconcile the past with the Lord, in Christian counseling, if necessary, to move forward. A redeemed woman need not be ashamed of a forgiven past. As Jesus said to the sinful woman, once your faith has saved you, you can go forth in peace.

Luke 7:48, 50
Then Jesus said to the woman, "Your sins are forgiven."
.. And Jesus said to the woman, "Your faith has saved you; go in peace."

Current life challenges may also prevent women from taking on mentoring roles. Trials tend to elicit questions and doubts about God's faithfulness, purposes and Sovereignty, leaving many Godly women to feel they ought not teach or train until they have all the answers. It is always wise to use discernment when mentoring intentionally in the midst of a trial, but the trial (in and of itself) isn't always a reason to hold back from mentoring and teaching opportunities.

When should you step back?

At a number of points in my mentoring journey, I have stepped back from actively mentoring and teaching. In one particular season of despair affected by many personal trials, the Lord made it quite clear that I was in no position to speak life into someone else's situation. My mentoring couch remained empty for nearly two years. Not only were girls not coming, I wasn't pursuing them nor making myself available for hosting ETC.

At times, I feared my influence was over, for good. I wondered if I'd ever have the joy of those special mentoring relationships. But I also recognized that I was unable to encourage others in the midst of my own mess. As I navigated through the difficulties and sought help from the Lord as well as through Christian counseling, the deep wounds in my soul were healed by God and I was able to move forward into healthy mentoring relationships.

The trial became a source of sanctification, bringing about a humility and compassion within me that I didn't have previously. Because of the pain endured and healing experienced, I brought to my relationships a new level of understanding, not only of the impact of sin but also the power of God's grace and freedom found in His forgiveness along with forgiving others.

> *Romans 8:28*
> *And we know that God causes everything to work together for the good of those who love God and are called according to his purpose for them.*

There are times in which mentoring ought to be put on hold for a season. This decision requires prayer, discernment and counsel from Godly advisors. We can always trust God's timing, both to reveal His purposes and to settle our uncertainty with His peace. We may not always have the answers to the "why" question, but we will be able to see how God transformed our pain into a beautiful testimony of His grace for His glory. At that point, it is certainly appropriate to share the story and engage actively in mentoring relationships.

When should you step in?

The enemy uses the fear of hypocrisy to undermine a woman's sphere of influence. But God has provided a perfect role model for us to follow as we seek to rebuke the enemy's lies: Paul was the biggest hypocrite of all time! He went from being a persecutor of Christ's followers to becoming persecuted for following Christ.

Paul's life was a mess before his conversion. He was a bold accuser of the followers of Jesus, and persecuted many for their faith. But once the scales on his eyes were removed, and his heart was totally yielded to the Lord, he became a great teacher and example for others. Because of Christ, Paul was equipped and qualified to teach, lead and mentor. His past did not disqualify him. Neither does ours. Paul set for us a model of how to live by seeking out the Savior's purposes.

> *1 Corinthians 11:1*
> *And you should imitate me, just as I imitate Christ.*

In 1 Corinthians 11:1, Paul teaches us to follow his example, because he is following the example of Christ. As mentors, we simply need to do the same. Sometimes, we simply need to step forward, in faith, pursuing mentoring relationships even when our history attempts to declare us unqualified. If the past has been reconciled and redeemed by God, we are perfectly qualified to speak Truth in the lives around us.

Take Time to Train

1. Take time to read and reflect on Luke 7:36-50.
2. Who do you identify with in the passage?
3. What can you learn from these verses?
4. Can you pinpoint situations from your past in which the enemy uses to call you a hypocrite? Take the time to seek the Lord's forgiveness and reconcile this past, as you move forward living as a forgiven woman. If you find yourself stuck in this process, see the help of your pastor or a Christian counselor.
5. Memorize 1 Corinthians 11:1 and use it to usher in a time of prayer.

~ • ~

CHAPTER SEVEN

But I'm Too Young!

As I look back on my journey from being twenty-something to thirty-something, I can think of a few key times in which a friend my age confessed, "I really want a mentor. I think I'm going to ask...if they would meet with me regularly." Each time, this comment struck me, as it seemed so unnatural to ask someone to become a mentor. I always thought it should be the older woman offering to mentor. Now that I am the older woman, it still feels awkward. I can't imagine going up to a younger woman and asking her if she wants to be mentored. I'd be too afraid I might insult her!

In hindsight, I can see that my perspective on mentoring had much to do with my independence and rebellious personality. I simply didn't want someone else to tell me how to live, even if I truly needed their help. By God's grace and intervention, He saw how desperately I needed the influence of older, wiser women, even if my pride was too great to seek it out. He brought women alongside me to speak words of encouragement, biblical insight and practical truth into my life. While I never experienced any formal mentoring relationships, I did experience the heart of mentoring through special friendships with older women. I recognize now how they seized key opportunities to set an example, guide me and respond to my curious questions about raising children, investing in my marriage, finding a routine and dealing with doubt about God's ways. Their influence was used by God to transform my heart, mind, soul and priorities.

Even though I didn't seek out a mentor, there were specific times in which I sought out advice. I remember one time asking an older friend,

Debbie, who had a beautifully maturing teenage daughter, about her parenting style. I really wanted to know how she managed to raise a polite, intelligent, creative, thoughtful girl in the midst of a culture that says it is impossible to do so in this day and age. Instead of giving me parenting advice, however, she introduced me to Anne Ortlund's book, *Disciplines of a Beautiful Woman*. Ortlund's trilogy literally changed my entire perspective on becoming the woman God intended, especially as a mother, wife and mentor, and radically influenced my approach in raising up our children. I no longer saw myself as a mother, but as a disciple of Christ commissioned to disciple others, beginning first with my children.

Ortlund's simple teaching awakened in me a brand new confidence in being able to learn Scripture, live it out and share it with others. God used *Disciplines* to set me on a journey of living intentionally,* and gave me eyes to see the mentoring already happening my life. I began to realize that mentoring happens naturally, in the way Titus 2 instructs, when we are trained by women in our lives, day-in and day-out, even if our relationship doesn't have a title or a scheduled meeting time.

This unintentional mentoring is exactly what occurred in a multigenerational way for my family through our interactions with our babysitters. From the time our first born was three months old, we took advantage of our boarding school community and brought into our home a teenage girl to babysit for our weekly date night. In the early years, I would pick a sitter that seemed to need a little bit of special attention, knowing my own kids would fill up her love tank and hopefully, I would have a chance to connect with her at the end of our date night and encourage her personally. Truly, my early mentoring experiences were shaped by these times with girls who our family still adores.

As our children grew, however, we became more intentional about looking for sitters who demonstrated a tenderness to our children as well as a sweet balance of maturity, teachability and sensitivity about their influence on our kids. When our oldest was entering the later part of elementary school, we were blessed with two precious young women who had a heart for God, an understanding of the times, and a deep love for our children. They were also eager to be mentored, and would stick around after we returned home from our date night to chat about our children as well as their share about their personal lives. Our sitters recognized early on that they needed mentors, and allowed me to fill that role. They also realized that even though they were young, they were in a position to mentor my own daughters. They used their babysitting opportunity to speak into my girls' lives, endearing their hearts to God's ways. By doing so, they became mentors at the young age of 16, using what I taught them each week to respond to the needs of the ones they delighted in mentoring.

> *1 Timothy 4:12*
> *Don't let anyone think less of you because you are young. Be an example to all believers in what you say, in the way you live, in your love, your faith, and your purity.*

Paul says we are never too young to set an example and embrace the call to mentor. As I witnessed firsthand in watching our teenage babysitters speak truth and wisdom into our lives (yes, even mine), I am convinced that age cannot disqualify you from mentoring. You can never be too young to impact others. You simply need to be sure you're influencing according to the Word. I beg you to not use the "I'm too young excuse" and miss out on the opportunity to be part of the ripple effect of one generation impacting another.

Take Time to Train

1. Is your pride keeping you from allowing older women to speak into your life?
2. Can you take a minute to look at your life to see if you've experienced informal mentoring? Jot down those moments and give thanks to the Lord for them.
3. Would you like to seek out a mentor? Who might you ask? Pray about this!
4. Is there a practical way you could informally mentor others?
5. Are there younger women that could use your influence? Write

down their names and pray about how God might like to use you.

You can find a large collection of living intentionally resources, inspired by Anne Ortlund and her writings, at http://www.elisapulliam.com/.

~ • ~

CHAPTER EIGHT

But I Lack Wisdom!

The fear of lacking wisdom is a common excuse for not answering the call to mentor. In our culture, where credibility and authority is determined by degrees and certificates, it is not surprising that many women feel it is not their place to speak into the lives of others. But biblical mentoring isn't about being a seminary graduate or appointed women's ministry leader. It is about knowing the Word, living it out and passing it on.

The "lack of wisdom" excuse is rooted in fear and anxiety. Women worry they might lead a mentoree down the wrong path with misguided advice. This is a legitimate concern which, if used appropriately, can make a mentor incredibly humble and approachable as opposed to self-righteous and arrogant. Mentoring is a serious and sacred undertaking! According to the Word, we are responsible for what we teach and how we speak into another person's life.

> *Matthew 12:36-37*
> *And I tell you this, you must give an account on judgment day for every idle word you speak. The words you say will either acquit you or condemn you.*

We are responsible for the words we speak. We will be held accountable for what we say. In James 3:1, we also learn that those who teach will be judged more strictly. We must evaluate our words so that truth is imparted but opinions are withheld, unless permission is granted to share our personal perspective a constructive way that illustrates the biblical principle at hand.

God equips us to mentor through giving wisdom to those who seek Him for it. In the same passage from James that warns us to be intentional, thoughtful, truth-filled teachers, we are also promised that the wisdom we need comes from above!

> *James 1:5*
> *If you need wisdom, ask our generous God, and he will give it to you. He will not rebuke you for asking.*

The Message translation of James 1:5 puts it this way, "If you don't know what you're doing, pray to the Father. He loves to help. You'll get his help, and He won't be condescended to when you ask for it." We don't need all the answers to life's great questions in order to validate our authority to mentor. We simply need to know where to find the answers: from God and through the Scriptures. This is summed up perfectly in Colossians:

> *Colossians 3:16*
> *Let the message about Christ, in all its richness, fill your lives. Teach and counsel each other with all the wisdom he gives. Sing psalms and hymns and spiritual songs to God with thankful hearts.*

Through our relationship with Christ and time spent in the Word, we are equipped by God to confidently and boldly mentor others. Feeling like we lack wisdom is not a valid excuse. Seeking the God who gives all wisdom is the answer!

Take Time to Train

1. Do you struggle with the fear of not being wise enough to mentor? If so, have you asked the Lord to impart His wisdom on you? If not, would you be willing to stop right now and pray about this matter?
2. Would you be willing to invest time in studying Scripture, so that the Word may dwell richly in you? If so, what first step could you take in that direction today?

3. Is there a Bible study you can get involved with at your church or online? If so, would you be willing to make that commitment today?
4. Would you be willing to set aside time each day to read the Word for twenty minutes, complete a Bible reading plan, and even listen to a sermon?

It is the desire of the ministry of *More to Be* to equip you with resources steeped in the Word. You can download Topics & Truth studies for free, here: http://www.moretobe.com/downloads/.

~ • ~

CHAPTER NINE

But It Is Not My Gifting!

Some women are great encouragers, finding opportunities to express simple but uplifting words with everyone they meet. Other women shine in serving a simple dinner party, preparing for a celebration, feeding the hungry at a soup kitchen, or hosting a main event at church. Some women are perfectly suited to organize every corner of their home and manage endless administrative details at work. There are also women passionate about Scripture, with a gift of teaching it to little ones and older ones alike. And there are women who have the gift of discernment, moving them to pray for the people God has put on their heart.

Within the family of God, women fill a vital role by using both their feminine qualities and God-given gifts to build one another up. The Word describes this process as each part being used for the benefit of the whole body of Christ. In 1 Corinthians 12:4-7, it is made clear that all these gifts are beneficial, but not necessarily the same.

> *1 Corinthians 12:4-7*
> *There are different kinds of spiritual gifts, but the same Spirit is the source of them all. There are different kinds of service, but we serve the same Lord. God works in different ways, but it is the same God who does the work in all of us. A spiritual gift is given to each of us so we can help each other.*

As women answering the call of mentoring the next generation, we need to avoid comparing ourselves to each other. God did not clone us. He didn't make one model good and another bad. He made us different and valuable. He made us to use our gifts and to be stretched beyond them. For example, every member of God's family is encouraged to practice hospitality, even if that isn't our primary spiritual gift (Romans 12:13).

We are created in the image of God, and we can bring to every relationship His purposes through freely using our gifts and talents. Every mentoring relationship, therefore, will look different, based on the God-designed uniqueness of each person.

To Biblically mentor simply means to live life, woman to woman, generation to generation, sharing what we are learning and passing it on to others. This is not a complicated, intricate process. It is simply about embracing and living out Paul's instructions in Philippians 4:

> *Philippians 4:8-9*
> *And now, dear brothers and sisters, one final thing. Fix your thoughts on what is true, and honorable, and right, and pure, and lovely, and admirable. Think about things that are excellent and worthy of praise. Keep putting into practice all you learned and received from me—everything you heard from me and saw me doing. Then the God of peace will be with you.*

As we seek to live a Godly life, modeled after biblical principles, we are being qualified by God to mentor others — so that the next generation may LEARN, RECEIVE, HEAR OR SEE in us and put into practice biblical principles. Our mentoring should reflect a natural overflow of our position in the body of Christ, as we pursue the things of Christ.

Ultimately, this idea of our unique position within the body of Christ also implies that we ought to have many mentors, because one woman could never meet all our needs to be trained up. Likewise, we should be joining other women, simultaneously mentoring the next generation together while operating within our own, unique gift set.

Take Time to Train

1. What do you see as the God-given gifts you bring to the body of Christ?
2. How could you use those gifts in a practical way in a mentoring relationship?
3. Take a few minutes to read all of 1 Corinthians 12 and Romans 12.
4. What instructions do you take away from these passages for using your gifts and stretching beyond them?
5. To consider how to practically understand and use your spiritual gifts, in the body of Christ and in your mentoring relationships, download the Topics & Truth lesson, A Look At Spiritual Gifts & Personality Types.
6. Who could you partner with in simultaneously mentoring the next generation?

~ • ~

CHAPTER TEN

But!

We've spent the previous chapters looking at the many excuses that stand in the way of mentoring. Actually, they are the same excuses that prevent us from becoming the women God intended:

Women who know whose they are and who they are.

Women who recognize the Sovereignty of God and find satisfaction in His provisions.

Women who face trials and challenges but emerge victorious and peace-filled.

Women who seek after God instead of others and other things.

When it comes right down to it, mentoring is about living as a disciple of Christ. Whether as a woman or a mentor, we will face challenges that cause us to doubt the call to live a life of influence. Even if we have fought hard against all the excuses we've looked at thus far, there still may be more that can derail us from answering the call to mentor...derailing you from experiencing life transformed, as God intended.

This "one more excuse" is the biggest of them all because it is completely and utterly yours. Only you will be able to uncover it and call it out, because it is so deeply rooted in your very own variety of insecurity, usually layered in jealousy and masked by a bit of arrogant perfectionism. Only you will be able to see it's ugly presence, as you pause to listen to the voices of doubt whispering defeat into your mind. You might hear it in that moment when you look outward instead of upward, and fall onto the slippery slope of "well, she has... does...is..."or find yourself repeating the mantra of "I don't...won't... can't...never will." This gruesome comparison cycle keeps women, like you and me, from seeing value in their own unique gifts, talents, personality, circumstances and purposes, while placing an inordinate value on someone else's.

So, we have to ask the difficult question: What is your but?

> But my house is too small...
> But my home isn't pretty enough...
> But my family is such a mess...
> But I'm not am not beautiful enough to stand in front of people...
> But what about the way I struggle with knowing what to say...
> But I know I'm not organized enough to be helpful...
> But my life is in chaos and I can't seem to make heads or tails of any of anything...
> But if I was married...
> But if I wasn't divorced...
> But if I had my own children...
> But if my prodigal child would come home...
> But I don't think she would ever want to talk to me...
> But!

We all have excuses.

What's yours?

More importantly, what does God have to say about it?

Take Time to Train

1. Pick out the key words or theme in your "but" excuse. Prayerfully lay these excuses at the cross and ask the Lord to speak His truth

into your situation.
2. Read Philippians 4:13 and bring each excuse to the Lord in prayer.
3. Continue to seek the Lord and study the Word to find out the truth that counters the lie connected to your excuse.
4. Download the Topics & Truth lesson, Mental Makeover, to understand further how your beliefs affect your actions.

~ • ~

CHAPTER ELEVEN

It Is Not About Me

Likely, the most influential Scripture passage that captures the essence of mentoring is Titus 2:3-5, which we've been referring to throughout the previous chapters. However, before we press on in discovering how simple mentoring truly is, we need to look closer at the meaning behind Titus 2 and why it is a foundational principle.

> *Titus 2:3-5*
> *Similarly, teach the older women to live in a way that honors God. They must not slander others or be heavy drinkers. Instead, they should teach others what is good. These older women must train the younger women to love their husbands and their children, to live wisely and be pure, to work in their homes, to do good, and to be submissive to their husbands. Then they will not bring shame on the word of God.*

According to this passage, how we live directly influences the impact we have on others, especially the next generation. Paul urges Titus to teach women to consider their day-in-day-out lives, because it is in doing life together that we carry the greatest level of influence. Paul begins the instruction warning about the temptations that women will face, knowing full well the ripple effect of sin. Yes, we are tempted to talk too much, and all too easily fall into slander. James 3 hones in on this principle, explaining how the tongue can destroy.

> *James 3:5-6*
> *In the same way, the tongue is a small thing that makes grand speeches. But a tiny spark can set a great forest on fire. And the tongue is a flame of fire. It is a whole world of wickedness, corrupting your entire body. It can set your whole life on fire, for it*

is set on fire by hell itself.

Paul also points out that we, as women, may stumble into addictions. In this case, he warns against drinking too much wine, an easily accessible feel-good drug, then and now. What do you think he would offer us as a word of caution today? I immediately think of how we use shopping, food and social media in unhealthy ways to numb out and illicit a high.

The teaching from Titus isn't only filled with warnings to stay away from drinking and gossip, but more importantly to focus on what is good. Paul encourages this particular focus, as he urges Titus to remind women to live out the Word so that we can train the next generation. Herein lies the mentoring principle we are guided by:

We mentor biblically as we follow Christ distinctly.

I believe that Paul offers this admonishment of how we are to live and who we are to train (our daughters, nieces, neighbors, women in the family of God) because of our tendency toward distraction. There are always more enticing pursuits! It isn't that we are prone to failing as wives, mothers, and home-keepers, but rather those relationships and responsibilities require much focus and discipline, undergirded by the pursuit of Christ wholly.

Paul understands the weakness of a woman, which I believe is a result of what he witnessed amongst the people he served. He saw the need for women to be intentionally self-controlled and pure, and so he offers that reminder. Wouldn't you agree that we need to be challenged in this area, too? We must resist the impulsive urge to buy or binge. We need to run from the drama on the TV and fill our minds with the things of Christ instead. We need to guard our thoughts as much as our bodies, being keenly aware of the temptations to sin. Again, this focus on being wise, or self-controlled, and pure is about the example we are setting through the life we are living.

Although it may be difficult to embrace this passage, we must take the whole of Scripture to heart. That means when the Word says we are to work in our homes, we need to investigate the implications of this instruction. Does it mean to never rest? No. Does it mean we shouldn't work outside of the home? Personally, I don't think so, although many scholars might disagree on this matter. I tend to lean to the translation which suggests this instruction is about the "caring for our homes." As women, it is a responsibility and a privilege to care for the home in which we live and the one in which we house our family. We don't need to make an idol of our housekeeping or master the art of interior decorating, but yet we should not neglect our dwelling place. Caring for our home is an opportunity to train up the next generation in how to do the same, with a focus on stewarding the provisions of God.

Why Paul chose to insert "to do good" in this passage may be even more puzzling than the call to be wise, pure and work at our home. Shouldn't that be obvious to all of us. However, if Paul thought it necessary and God ordered it in His Word, we must heed it. Do good. Yes, our rebellious and selfish nature will wrestle against this instruction with flesh-driven fits and lazy-girl distractions. But how can we teach and train if our actions repulses those we're called to influence?

Finally, Paul urges us to be submissive to our husbands. Now before you object, consider the heart of this issue. To be submissive, which is also translated as obedient or subject, riles up many women with a tremendously negative connotation. Paul, however, is not suggesting that females are second class citizens to be ruled and managed. He is however, reminding us of the fall, where God declared that a woman would desire to rule over her husband. When humankind was turned upside down by the stinking-apple-eating-incident, the order of things also went awry. In Christ, however, it doesn't have to stay that way. By the power of the Holy Spirit working within a woman, she could discern her rebellious desire to dominate her husband and choose to not give into the temptation. This does not mean that a man ought to dominate his wife. On the contrary, Ephesians 5:21 1 calls both husband and wife into submission to one another in reverence for Christ. Ultimately, if a wife is married to a man who is living out the Ephesians 5 call, submitting to him as unto the Lord is a beautiful gift that is given, not demanded, from a woman.

How we live can either honor God and promote His word, or utterly and completely malign it. That's a sobering thought! If what we do negatively impacts someone, and specifically causes them to find Jesus or the Bible distasteful, then we have brought shame on the Word of God. The truth is that how we live either impacts others for Christ or turns them away. This doesn't mean we need to be perfect, because that is impossible. But it does mean we ought to live humbly, with a contrite heart and desire to please God by obeying His word.
With a Titus 2 perspective in mind, we can honestly say that biblical mentoring isn't really about how I feel. It is not about me. It is not about you. It is about them. The ones we long to influence.

Biblical mentoring is about living out God's word in such a way that our lives impact the next generation for God's glory.

As we seek to apply the principles of Titus 2, as well as the many other passages we've considered thus far, our focus must be on mentoring biblically as we follow Christ distinctly. It is a privilege to answer the call to mentor by setting a biblical example for the women in our lives — older, younger, daughter, niece, sister, mother, friend and stranger alike. It is in these primary relationships that we must be intentional and purposed in how we respond to the Word. There isn't a format or a program that we must follow in order to make this happen, but rather normal routines that ebb and flow throughout our days in which we grab moments to train up the next generation.

Once we establish a lifestyle of mentoring naturally, launching into a formal mentoring relationship or beginning a mentoring ministry, such as ETC, Mug & Mornings, or Grace Chats, is an ideal next step. Instead of putting on a mentoring program, we simply extend from our home life a natural safe-haven for others to learn from our example and benefit from purposeful instruction. We mentor by doing life according to Scripture with the women God puts in our family, friendships, church, work and neighborhood.

Take Time to Train

The first portion of this journey has focused heavily on the philosophy and biblical foundation of the call to impact the next generation through mentoring. It is a lot to digest! Take time now to pray and journal about what you've learned thus far and to prepare your heart for the practical points that will come in the next portion of this adventure.

Heavenly Father, thank you for this journey.

I'm intrigued by these new ideas...

Please help me to see how what I'm learning fits into my life...

Lord, give me a clear understanding of what you expect of me, so that I may live in that sweet place of obedience and grace...

Lord, thank you for the opportunity to learn and grow and become the woman you intended, so that I may glorify You in all that I say and do.

In Jesus' Strong Name, Amen.

~ • ~

PART THREE

M.E.N.T.O.R.I.N.G.

Young women today are learning about character and holiness from mainstream fashion and lifestyle magazines. To our shame, Christian women are sitting comfortably in soft pews in whitewashed churches and allowing the world to teach its values to our young women. We, the body and bride of Christ, should be the ones teaching our young women how to be women of faith who believe in the one true God; women who exhibit noble character and holiness before God. This is our calling in this generation.

Leah Adams
From the Trash Pile to the Treasure Chest: Creating a Godly Legacy

CHAPTER TWELVE

Like A Baton Pass

Mentoring is like a baton pass in a relay race involving one generation to the next. As one woman receives from the Lord, she in turn refreshes another, passing the baton of her faith and biblical wisdom to another.

Ultimately, mentoring is extending out your hand into her hand to place it into God's hand, and it can happen in the context of many different types of relationships, such as:

- mother to daughter
- grandma to grand-daughter
- seasoned ministry leader to new ministry leader
- Bible study teacher to a new group attendee
- twenty-something college junior to an incoming freshman
- thirty-something new mom to a neighborhood teen
- a tween momma's helper to a toddler, if you can imagine

Sometimes these relationships are fostered by blood and proximity in doing life together, other times they are arranged by a divinely timed calendar and occasion. Regardless of the dynamic, mentoring relationships are both a privilege and responsibility. As such, having a clear set of expectations, boundaries and goals will bring out a healthy, beneficial result.

Simply put, mentoring involves these key aspects:

1. **Meeting**

2. **Encouraging**
3. **Noticing**
4. **Teaching**
5. **Offering**
6. **Responding**
7. **Inspiring**
8. **Navigating**
9. **Growing**

In the following chapters, we're going to discover the ways to make mentoring simple and effective, enabling you to step out as a disciple of Christ to influence and impact others for His glory. Each step along the way, I encourage you to devote time to pray, asking God to direct your steps and confirm His call on your life in the area of intentionally mentoring. If you haven't already set aside a notebook for the journey, I encourage you to do so now, so that you'll have a place to record the many ideas the Lord will bring your way.

Take Time to Train

1. What do you think of these key words in relationship to the idea of mentoring?
2. Which ones do you look forward to unpacking?
3. Which ones make you a bit nervous?
4. Take time to pray for God to open your mind to receiving His perspective on the mentoring call.

~ • ~

CHAPTER THIRTEEN

Meeting

The "M" in mentoring stands for spending time together by meeting with one another in whatever way the Lord provides and leads. In practical terms, this will take on a different format depending on the mentoring relationship. In each case, however, there are creative ways to make the most of your time meeting together and to set up healthy boundaries for a successful mentoring experience.

Prayer

Before committing to meeting with a mentoree, set aside time to pray for the relationship and the Lord's direction. I encourage you to pray before and after every meeting time, asking the Lord to ordain every word that will be spoken and every experience shared as well as to bind up the work of the enemy. It is also be wise for you to seek godly counsel and confirmation about embarking on a mentoring relationship, while you are still in the praying stage.

Time

Look ahead at your schedule and set aside a particular time each week to meet for intentional mentoring. Even if the relationship is between mom and daughter, where mentoring happens daily, it is still wise to set apart this time. As you consider when you'll be meeting together, also define the length of time of each appointment.

Place

Pick an agreed upon place for mentoring, where you will both be free from distractions. A home is a great setting, and allows for intimacy and creativity, but if people are bouncing around and the phone is ringing off the hook, it might be better to opt for a walk or getting together at a favorite coffee place.

Format

In some cases, meeting face-to-face isn't possible for a mentoring relationship. If this is your situation, decide on what other communication option is viable, such as phone, text messaging, Skype, Facebook chat, or even through email. Think outside of the box to find what works best for both of you.

Purpose

It is a great idea to set a tentative plan for what you'll be doing in your time together. If you don't have a purpose for your mentoring relationship, it is easy to grow discouraged and distracted. While your purpose doesn't have to be irrevocable, it is a good idea to agree upon the reason you'll be devoting time to meeting together. Consider these options for your mentoring purpose:

- Prayer
- Accountability
- Study of Scripture
- Discussing a particular issue

- Reading a book together
- Honing in on a life skill

Boundaries

When a mentoring relationship takes on a formal dynamic through a regular meeting time, it becomes very important to set boundaries to avoid bitterness and conflict later on. Together, you should determine and agree upon the following:

- length of each meeting, such as 45 minutes to an hour
- how often you will meet, such as once a week or every other week
- how long you'll meet for, such as three to six months
- purpose of your meeting time
- confidentiality, as in what is shared is kept private unless it is a matter of emotional or physical crisis that requires medical or legal attention
- commitment expectation, such as cancellations must be 24 hours in advance
- a date to reevaluate and set a new mentoring course

Permission

If you will be mentoring a young person, be sure to receive their parent(s) or guardians permission. It is wise to inform them of your intentions and request the support of your mentoring relationship. In most cases, they will be delighted to have your investment of time and love in their child's life.

Meeting with your mentoree will become one of those treasured opportunities as you see God's hand orchestrating the details of your lives and weaving your stories together.

Take Time to Train

1. How could you practically incorporate these ideas in your current mentoring relationship, in particular with your own daughter?
2. How do these ideas redefine the nuts and bolts of mentoring in your mind?
3. Which of these practical ideas will come naturally to you?
4. Which one(s) make you uncomfortable and will present a challenge?
5. Consider reading Boundaries, by Cloud and Townsend for an overview of what it looks like to have healthy relationships.

~ • ~

CHAPTER FOURTEEN

Encouraging

The "E" in mentoring is all about encouraging one another through words and deeds that glorify God. The way you go about encouraging your mentoree will be unique to your combination of gifts, talents, experiences, personality and love language. The way your mentoree receives your gifts of encouragement can be equally diverse. However, for every mentoring relationship, the focus on encouragement should be practical and steeped in biblical truth and principles.

Encourage Practically

As you look for opportunities to encourage your mentoree, begin with a discovery of her love languages, as taught by Gary Chapman. Simply by looking at how she receives love and how she naturally gives it, will offer great conversation starters and very specific steps for following up with her in the weeks and months ahead. In addition, you might want to look into doing a personality profile with her, which will enable you both to communicate with a greater measure of sensitivity for each other's God-given conversation style.

Words
Does she like to have the opportunity to talk? Is she encouraged by words of affirmation? How often does she need to connect with you verbally to be confident about your relationship?

Time
Does she feel loved by time being spent together? How much time is enough in her mind? Who else is she craving time with?

Gifts
Does she respond to gifts? Does the price tag matter? Is it the personalization that grabs her heart?

Touch
How does she feel about being hugged? Does she like it when you pat her on the back or gently encourage her with squeeze of the hand?

Actions
What actions demonstrate love to her? Is she looking to co-labor with you in the kitchen or on a walk? Does serving one another speak love to her?

Encourage Biblically

The Scriptures are rich in instruction on how to navigate through relationships. God has been gracious to remind us how to speak to one another, serve each other and season our conversations with words of encouragement. Simply by applying these few Scripture passages, you can set the tone for your relationship so that you encourage her using biblical principles.

What should we talk about?

Philippians 4:8-9 "And now, dear brothers and sisters, one final thing. Fix your thoughts on what is true, and honorable, and right, and pure, and lovely, and admirable. Think about things that are excellent and worthy of praise. Keep putting into practice all you learned and received from me—everything you heard from me and saw me doing. Then the God of peace will be with you."

How should I love her?

1 Corinthians13 MSG "The Way of Love. If I speak with human eloquence and angelic ecstasy but don't love, I'm nothing but the creaking of a rusty gate. If I speak God's Word with power, revealing all his mysteries and making everything plain as day, and if I have faith that says to a mountain, "Jump," and it jumps, but I don't love, I'm nothing. If I give everything I own to the poor and even go to the stake to be burned as a martyr, but I don't love, I've gotten nowhere. So, no matter what I say, what I believe, and what I do, I'm bankrupt without love. Love never gives up. Love cares more for others than for self. Love doesn't want what it doesn't have. Love doesn't strut, Doesn't have a swelled head, Doesn't force itself on others, Isn't always "me first," Doesn't fly off the handle, Doesn't keep score of the sins of others, Doesn't revel when others grovel, Takes pleasure in the flowering of truth, Puts up with anything, Trusts God always, Always looks for the best, Never looks back, But keeps going to the end. Love never dies. Inspired speech will be over some day; praying in tongues will end; understanding will reach its limit. We know only a portion of the truth, and what we say about God is always incomplete. But when the Complete arrives, our incompletes will be canceled."

How should I use the word?

2 Timothy 4:2 "Preach the Word; be prepared in season and out of season; correct, rebuke and encourage—with great patience and careful instruction."

How should I respond to her?

What should I do when things are not going well?
James 1:19 "Understand this, my dear brothers and sisters: You must all be quick to listen, slow to speak, and slow to get angry."

What should I do if she has hurt me?

Colossians 3:12-15 " Since God chose you to be the holy people he loves, you must clothe yourselves with tenderhearted mercy,

> kindness, humility, gentleness, and patience. Make allowance for each other's faults, and forgive anyone who offends you. Remember, the Lord forgave you, so you must forgive others. Above all, clothe yourselves with love, which binds us all together in perfect harmony. And let the peace that comes from Christ rule in your hearts. For as members of one body you are called to live in peace. And always be thankful."

There are so many wonderful ways you can practically and biblically encourage your mentoree. As the ideas come to you, take the time to jot them down and pray through the opportunities to offer rich encouragement to those you mentor.

Take Time to Train

1. What do you think your love language is? How can your awareness of your love language integrate into your current relationships?
2. Can you think of one action step that would be received as encouragement for each of the five different love languages?
3. Looking at the Scripture passages, jot down a list of action words and descriptive adjectives to create a checklist for your mentoring relationships.

~ • ~

CHAPTER FIFTEEN

Noticing

The "N" in mentoring stands for noticing your mentoree, which is about a whole lot more than simply looking at her. It means paying attention to her life and asking questions to discover what is happening in her heart.

Yes, noticing requires observation, as her body language will speak volumes in revealing how she's really doing. But it also requires intentionality and a keen ear to listen for both what she says and doesn't say. As you approach your meeting time with your mentoree, keep these noticing reminders in the forefront of your mind:
Through your time together, whether it is face to face, over the phone, or through the written word such as text or email, actively listen and look for opportunities to come alongside, encourage, pray and respond to her practical needs, both in the moment and in the future.

- Listen for dates, such as anniversaries and birthdays of loved ones, in which you can mark on your calendar and send a card, email or text message.
- Make a note of upcoming events that need extra prayer and support, such as an interview, conference, travel or event, and be sure to call on that day.
- Discern if she is overwhelmed by going someplace alone or getting ready for an event, and offer her companionship.
- Prod beyond her words, asking questions to reveal the true state of her heart, and then offer to pray together.
- How does she look today? Run down, distracted, stressed? Put

your agenda for your meeting time on hold and ask how she's doing. Be willing to change up your time to give her some refreshment.

We all like to be noticed. Especially when it comes from a heart of compassion and concern. Noticing your mentoree and responding to her "state" is key to offering her personalized and practically encouragement.

Take Time to Train

1. How do you feel when someone takes time to notice you? How are you encouraged by a comment or action that responds to how you are doing personally? In what ways have you been hurt by the lack of noticing happening in your life?
2. Are you sensitive to listening beyond someone's words to decode the story of the heart? If not, try practicing this skill on friends and family, looking beyond the words to hearing what exactly they are hiding or holding within.
3. Do you sometimes feel uncertain how to respond to someone else's problems? Take time now to ask God to give you the ability to listen well and pray it up, instead of feeling compelled to fix everything.

~ • ~

CHAPTER SIXTEEN

Teaching

The "T" in mentoring stands for teaching and it incorporates both the practical aspect of teaching the Word and also going beyond in training up a mentoree in life skills. According to Titus 2:3-5, it is clearly within the responsibilities of older women to teach the younger generation how to live. This teaching may encompass many different areas of life, such as a home-keeper, wife, mother and disciple. In a biblical mentoring relationship, teaching may take on the shape of a conversation and discussion or look like a side-by-side experience of training through time spent together, such as the following:

- Spending a Saturday afternoon teaching your daughter or mentoree how to care for a home.
- Inviting a younger woman over from church to plant a garden.
- Asking for companionship from a college girls on a shopping trip with the little ones.
- Planning and hosting a holiday party or gathering and teaching your mentoree every step of the process.
- Setting aside time to teach the basics of finances and managing a budget.
- Purging her closet, making new outfits, and even teaching a few makeup techniques.

Teaching a mentoree may also be focused on studying the Word, focusing on a portion of Scripture or on a particular topic using a book, resource or the Topics & Truth Free Downloads available at www.moretobe.com. This particular list of books are ideal to add to your mentoring library and to consider using in a short-term study with a mentoree:

- *Disciplines Of The Beautiful Woman*, Anne Ortlund
- *Lord, Teach Me to Pray in 28 Days*, Kay Arthur
- *Discerning the Voice of God: How to Recognize When God Speaks*, Priscilla Shirer
- *Grace for the Good Girl: Letting Go of the Try-Hard Life*, Emily P. Freeman

Sharing the Word, along with teaching practical life lessons, is a wonderful gift to pass on to a mentoree. Whether she is your daughter, niece, neighbor, or friend, she will be incredibly grateful and you will be blessed by the opportunity to serve in this way.

Take Time to Train

1. Have you thought about building a mentoring library? Begin yours today by printing out the *Topics & Truth Free Downloads* and putting them in a binder to start your collection.
2. What are some of the practical skills you could pass onto a mentoree? Consider what skills are unique to your personality and upbringing, lifestyle habits or experiences, which you could focus on teaching to others.
3. What area of life would you like to receive teaching in? Spend time today looking for those resources and opportunities.

~ • ~

CHAPTER SEVENTEEN

Offering

The "O" in mentoring presents a challenge to consider practical ways to serve your mentoree as you offer your time, talents and resources in your spiritual act of worship unto the Lord. According to Romans 12:1, Paul instructs believers to live in such a way that our lives become beautiful, holy and pleasing sacrifices unto God.

> *Romans 12:1*
> *And so, dear brothers and sisters, I plead with you to give your bodies to God because of all he has done for you. Let them be a living and holy sacrifice—the kind he will find acceptable. This is truly the way to worship him.*

This act of becoming a living sacrifice is true worship, as much as being in church on Sunday morning and belting out praise songs. It is a daily discipline of using our God-given gifts, talents, relationships, circumstances and opportunities to praise God and serve Him in the moment.

To live in the mindset of worship is a beautiful thing, but not always easy. It requires turning our eyes and ears toward the Lord, and tuning our mind and heart toward the Holy Spirit's promptings. It is the choice to give thanks and praise, instead of complaining. To sacrifice and serve, instead of growing bitter. To put off and put on hold, instead of pushing ahead. To lay down your agenda, for the sake of meeting a real need in someone else's life.

In your biblical mentoring relationship, it is vital to both model a Romans 12:1 life as well as give it as a gift to your mentoree. As she witnesses how you respond to the Holy Spirit's leading, considering your unique circumstances and relationships, she will learn how to be molded by the Lord's purposes and plans for her days.

This idea of a Romans 12 life requires the gentle balance of boundaries in the context of being led by the Holy Spirit. Whether you are offering your gifts, talents and time to your mentoree, or if she is simply witnessing how you do this with your family, she will learn how to serve others as a spiritual act of worship and yield her life to the Lord in a beautiful offering.

Take Time to Train

1. Have you ever considered life as a spiritual act of worship?
2. Do you find it a challenge to serve others with a good attitude? Why or why not?
3. What next step could you take toward living with a Romans 12:1 mindset?
4. Seek the Lord on this today, carving out 12 minutes to pray about this one very important biblical principle. Then see if you can write down 12 simple responsibilities in which you could focus on doing with a spiritual act of worship mindset.

~ • ~

CHAPTER EIGHTEEN

Responding

The "R" in mentoring stands for responding to your mentoree's life and circumstances. It requires an attentive eye and sensitive heart, to see both the practical and spiritual needs in her life. Through times in conversation, prayer and companionship, you should purposefully ask the Holy Spirit to give you a discernment in knowing how and when to respond to her real, felt needs and spiritual needs.

As a biblical mentor, you are more than just a cheerleader and teacher, encourager and companion. You are also an accountability partner, making it vitally important that you share the Truth, and not only what will make her feel good. You don't want to tickle her ears with false hopes and empty promises.

Responding to her needs and circumstances is a heavy responsibility, which must come under the authority of Scripture. At times, your mentoree is simply going to be a mess, heading down the wrong road of thinking and potentially landing on the wrong path of destruction. That's exactly when you will need to speak the truth in love and be bold in keeping healthy boundaries. She needs your commitment to the Word and your unwavering love to support her ability to be obedient to the Lord, now more than ever. It is natural for her to challenge your authority in her life and manipulate your emotions, but do your best to not yield to her pressure by getting support from wiser, older women and even your pastor or spouse.

The Word promises that Truth spoken in love is the source of growth, so seize opportunities to respond to your mentoree's life in the pleasant times with an outpouring of Scripture training. When you return to the Word during difficult times, it will be less of shock and more of a comfort to her, because of the foundation of Scripture already established in her life and your relationship.

Most importantly, pause for prayer before speaking a single word in response to your mentoree's needs. Ask the Lord for His Spirit to lead you and strengthen you, as you invest tangibly in her spiritual growth.

Take Time to Train

1. How do you feel about responding to your mentoree in the difficult times as well as the good times?
2. What makes you afraid of these strained relationships moments? How might you gain the strength and boldness to speak the truth in love?
3. Spend time in prayer, asking God to give you a sensitivity to the Holy Spirit's leading in your life, especially in your mentoring relationships.
4. Take time to look up and reflect upon the following Scriptures: Hebrews 4:12, Ephesians 4:15, Ephesians 4:25, 1 Corinthians 2:13, John 16:13.
5. Prayerfully ask God for the ways you can implement these truths in all your relationships.
6. Which one(s) should you commit to memory?
7. Which one(s) could you teach and share with the next generation today?

~ • ~

CHAPTER NINETEEN

Inspiring

The "I" in mentoring stands for inspiring. Now before this idea intimidates you, let me show you how simple it is to become a source of inspiration to your mentoree. According to the dictionary, to inspire means "to exert a stimulating or beneficial effect upon (a person); animate or invigorate; stir; to prompt or instigate; give rise to; to guide or arouse by divine influence or inspiration." When you stop to think about it, there really could be no better definition to describe the role of a mentor.

As a woman, living life as a disciple of Christ, you are an inspiration to those around you. You inspire by your faith in action. You inspire by the risks you take on behalf of those you life. You inspire as you use your gifts and talents for the glory of God. You inspire simply by being a child of God, loving and worshipping the one who made you in His image.

Inspiring others is not about proving one's accomplishments nor conquering her daily responsibilities at home, work, church. It isn't about perfecting relationships and mastering her roles as wife, mom, or friend. Inspiring someone else is about living as an example of humility, perseverance, and purpose.
When a woman arises each morning, established in her identity as a daughter of the King, with a fresh desire to live for God's glory, she is inspiring to the next generation.

Paul captures the essence of living an inspiring life in his letter to the Thessalonians. He writes:

1 Thessalonians 1:3
As we pray to our God and Father about you, we think of your faithful work, your loving deeds, and the enduring hope you have because of our Lord Jesus Christ.

The Thessalonians lived in such a way that their work was produced by their faith. Faith came first. Their ongoing labor was prompted by love. And their endurance was inspired by the hope they had in the Lord Jesus Christ. As a woman, this is how you can live in such a way to inspire others. As a biblical mentor, this is a blueprint for wisely approaching mentoring relationships. Each one, whether intentional or casual, should be established because of your faith in Christ and sustained by His love. As you live inspired by the hope of Jesus in your life, you will, in turn, inspire those you mentor to do the same.

Take Time to Train

1. Can you think of one or two women that have inspired you to become the woman God intended, even if you did not have a close or personal relationship with them?
2. How did they accomplish that noble act of inspiring you?
3. How can you do that for the younger women in your life?
4. Take the time to look up 1 Thessalonians 3:4-10. Read through it once, slowly. Return to the passage a second time and look for the instruction and application for yourself, and in your role as a mentor. Journal about what it means to be chosen by God, and how you can live as an imitator of Christ in a practical way for others to witness and be inspired in their own life and faith journey.

~ • ~

CHAPTER TWENTY

Navigating

The "N" in mentoring stands for navigating. As a biblical mentor, you want to come alongside the younger women God has positioned in your life and help them navigate their way through life, holding firmly onto biblical principles. As Jesus teaches in Matthew 7, we want to help our mentorees choose the narrow road for their life journey, and to stay off the broad road that leads to destruction.

> *Matthew 7:13-14 ESV*
> *Enter by the narrow gate. For the gate is wide and the way is easy that leads to destruction, and those who enter by it are many. For the gate is narrow and the way is hard that leads to life, and those who find it are few.*

Likely, we know what the easy road looks like. It is marked off by the wide gate that we've bumped into maybe once, or maybe one too many times. It opens wide to the destructive path, one that we might have walked on in our life journey. It is the way of the crowd. It is often the culturally popular road.

As mentors, we have the opportunity to stand at that wide gate and shout, "Turn! Don't go this way! Please heed this instruction!" Yes, we can share our stories and offer our wisdom, bathed in prayer and washed with the Word. We can beckon and encourage our mentoree to position herself on the narrow road that leads to life. We can point out that small gate and encourage that step of faith toward a better future. The Scriptures say only a few find the narrow gate. Is that because it takes a careful eye to see it? Possibly. Or maybe that is because it also requires a more determined step?

At each turn of your mentoree's life, she will have a choice to make. As you journey with her, your goal is to offer your wisdom, experience and biblical truth to help her to navigate her course. You stand at the crossroads awaiting for her, doing all the things a mentor does (meeting, encouraging, noticing, teaching, offering, responding, inspiring), but with open hands raised toward the cross.

When it comes down to making the decision, you won't be the one to do it. You can't make her walk through the gate. You can't put her on the narrow road. She needs to decide for herself and you need to give her permission to do so. If she ends up on the wrong path, you can be the one she runs to when she decides to turn the other way...ready to put her life right into Jesus' arms.

Take Time to Train

1. What do you think would be your personal greatest challenge in waiting at the crossroads for a mentoree who is heading down the broad path?
2. Considering your potential situation, how can you prepare yourself now to navigate through that time?
3. How have your past mistakes that landed you on the wide path been reconciled and redeemed by God? If you have not worked through your past, make an appointment with God to do so soon. If needed, see a Christian counselor to help you work through the healing process so that you may move forward unhindered by the baggage from you past.
4. Spend time in prayer, seeking the Lord for His perspective as you prepare to mentor others.

~ • ~

CHAPTER TWENTY-ONE

Growing

We've finally come to our last letter in our mentoring acronym. "G" in mentoring stands for growing in faith, with grace, together.

> *2 Thessalonians 1:3 NIV*
> *Dear brothers and sisters, we can't help but thank God for you, because your faith is flourishing and your love for one another is growing.*

The mentoree isn't the only one growing in the Lord. Every biblical mentor should also be maturing in her personal faith. This requires a personal commitment to Scripture study, times of prayer, discussing biblical principles with peers, sitting under the teaching of seasoned pastors and Bible study leaders, learning new aspects of theology, serving others with a heart for God's kingdom purposes, and applying the truths found in Scripture to every day life. This type of spiritual growth should not only be modeled but also practically encouraged.

Your goal as a mentor is for you to live out your faith and inspire your mentoree to become confident in her own faith walk. While you may heavily focus on training her in the disciplines of being a godly woman, the end result is always because of the work of the Holy Spirit. You are not the one making her grow. Your role is to be a co-laborer with God, first and foremost through prayer, and second, by showing the love of God to her in action and in word, as you speak to the truth to her time and time again.

Colossians 1:9-12
So we have not stopped praying for you since we first heard about you. We ask God to give you complete knowledge of his will and to give you spiritual wisdom and understanding. Then the way you live will always honor and please the Lord, and your lives will produce every kind of good fruit. All the while, you will grow as you learn to know God better and better.

We also pray that you will be strengthened with all his glorious power so you will have all the endurance and patience you need. May you be filled with joy, always thanking the Father. He has enabled you to share in the inheritance that belongs to his people, who live in the light.

While growing is a necessary part of every mentoring relationship, growing in grace is even more important. As in any relationship, there will be wonderful times of conversing and doing life together, and ugly moments of disappointment and difficulties. Grace is the healing balm necessary for all relationships.

Always. Grace.

Because biblical mentoring is messy. Yes, messy grace in action, as I like to call it. Circumstances and conversations aren't always pretty, especially when they require crossroad realities and hard core truths. Biblical mentoring also demands intentionality and focus, and sometimes that's not possible. A mentor is a real woman, with a real life. And sometimes life will get in the way of the ideal. It is not wrong when a woman's heart is committed to the relationship, but her life is unavoidably full, preventing her from making the investment of time she sincerely desires. It is equally possible for a mentor to have the initial desire to be present physically and emotionally, but as her life circumstances change, she finds her heart consumed by other matters and her mind distracted or preoccupied. These challenges present obstacles in the mentoring relationship and require a grace-filled response.

Grace to reevaluate without being offended.

Grace to present a new plan of action.

Grace to say, I'm simply not sufficient for your needs, but I know the One who is.

> *2 Corinthians 12:9 NIV*
> *But He said to me, "My grace is sufficient for you, for my power is made perfect in weakness." Therefore I will boast all the more gladly about my weaknesses, so that Christ's power may rest on me.*

For a mentoring relationship to grow in spiritual maturity, both together and individually, grace is a necessary ingredient. As you are pressed in upon and stretched beyond your human ability, grace will enable you to let the relationship take its God-ordained course, trusting His perfect plan for the growth necessary in each of your lives.

Take Time to Train

1. Would you say you are growing in your faith, personally?
2. If so, what is spurring you on in this direction? How can you share this reality with someone who might need encouragement to press on in their faith journey and the practice of spiritual disciplines?
3. If you are not growing in your faith, what is one step you can take in that direction?
4. Is there someone you can ask to hold you accountability in this action step?
5. What does God's grace mean to you?
6. How can you practice sharing God's grace with others?

~ • ~

PART FOUR

Make An Impact

Though we certainly need each other,
no one but God is indispensable.

Dr. Henry Cloud and Dr. John Townsend
Boundaries: When to Say YES and When to Say NO to Take Control of Your Life

CHAPTER TWENTY-TWO

Don't Forget the Tea

In the midst of all this training, have you forgotten why you embarked on this journey? It is so easy to get bogged down with details and to be easily distracted from the call to mentor by the realistic demands on your life. Let me offer you a grace moment. Forget everything I've shared with you except this one truth:

> **In order to mentor biblically we must first follow Christ distinctly.**

In other words, simply live as a follower of your Lord and Savior Jesus Christ, putting one foot in front of another, as you journey through the opportunities God gives you each day.

Sometimes, we get so caught up in a method or mission that we complicate the process and purpose. If you're caught in that place right now, take a minute to simply breathe. Give God the glory for all the ways He's already worked in your life. Recognize how far you've come, by His grace of course. Give the Lord His due praise for giving you the time, energy and discipline to even read this far in Impact My Life. What a tremendous accomplishment, friend!

The demands on our time are endless. As I write this, I have over 176 emails in my inbox awaiting my attention, and I usually keep my inbox empty of anything not pressing. There is no way I'll be able to take care of 176 requests for my attention, plus respond to the needs of the six children living in my home during this summer season, a husband who'd like to have a semiconscious wife to spend time with later this evening, a house crying out for a dust bunny war, a ministry website with five pending posts waiting to be approved, and, well, I could go on and on. I bet you can too.

Life happens.

But so does mentoring. Sometimes formally and sometimes casually.

But it can't happen without Christ.

You Need the Tea and the "T"!

The title of this chapter has a dual purpose: I want to encourage you to keep mentoring as simple as serving a cup of tea while also reminding you that you can't do anything, not even serve a cup of tea to a mentoree, without considering the cross of Christ.

My urging to "not forget the tea" is about a whole lot more than a collection of tea bags and a ceramic pot with a rooster on top. When I say "tea," I am also thinking "t," because this one little letter always reminds me of the cross.

The Blessing of a Tea Basket

As simple as this seems, the most practical thing you can do to set the tone for your mentoring relationships is fix yourself a tea basket and have it on hand at a moments notice. Grab a wicker basket from the dollar store, select a half dozen boxes of tea on sale at the local supermarket, discard the boxes and fill your basket to overflowing. Keep it stocked and even in sight. Why? Because the tea can remind you to run to the cross and spend time some high tea time with Jesus each afternoon, as one of my mentor friend's likes to make time for personally and corporately.

A hot cup of tea also makes one slow down to build relationships. When you pour a cup of tea for your mentoree, time is captured while waiting for your fresh brew to cool. She speaks and you listen. As she sips, you respond, gently and with prayed upon words of encouragement. Of course, if you don't like tea, sneak in some hot chocolate packets and even a few special instant coffee treats.

Having a tea basket on hand also makes hosting an ETC, Mugs & Muffins, or Grace Chats gathering super easy. In preparation for each meeting time, all you have to do is boil some water, grab a stack of hot cups, and position them on the kitchen counter with the tea basket. Making this little touch of hospitality a cinch will offer you more time to pray in preparation for your gathering and connect with your guests when they arrive.

The Power of the Cross

The cross is where Jesus conquered death and rose again. It is the symbol of our faith because it is where our relationship with God becomes a reality and our new birth in Christ a possibility. The cross is also a perfect reminder to us that Jesus is the only Savior anyone ever needs. The people you love don't need you as much as they need Jesus. You simply need to live each moment, humbly and boldly giving off the aroma of Christ because of your deep, authentic and life transforming personal relationship with your Redeemer (2 Corinthians 2:15). While serving tea may be the key to cultivating a warm and inviting setting for your mentorees to open up, it is truly the cross that holds the key to their heart and opens the door for them to experience life transformed.

I've promised to give you mentoring simplified, didn't I? And I honestly believe that embracing this idea of not forgetting the tea will enable you to move forward with confidence in your mentoring journey.

So, how about fixing your tea basket right now?

Take Time to Train

1. What's the first step you can take to assemble your tea basket?
2. Is there a deadline in which you'd like to have it ready?
3. Do you also need to include a cross somewhere in your home or gathering times to remind you to run to Jesus and invite others there too?
4. How about fixing yourself a cup of tea right now and spending the time it takes to sip it in prayer and quiet reflection with the Lord?

~ • ~

CHAPTER TWENTY-THREE

Focus. Find. Follow Through.

It is now time to get active in your mentoring pursuit. You've been given the foundational principles of biblical mentoring partnered with realistic expectations and healthy relationship building steps. I've simplified the process for you with a reminder to not forget the tea, meaning both the power of the cross and the benefit of a slow sipping drink. You are more than ready to take your first steps of faith into a lifestyle of mentoring by focusing, finding and following through on the opportunities God will provide for you. If you are like me, however, you might like a simple "to do list" to guide you in becoming an active mentor, so here is what I would recommend as your next steps:

Focus

Pray!

Pour out your heart to God concerning your desire to mentor. Ask the Lord for His perspective and direction, along with a steadfastness to keep your eyes on Him and to wait on His timing or to leap out in faith. If you like to keep a prayer journal, write out your thoughts and concerns as well as specific prayer needs. If you have a group of women who serve as your accountability or prayer partners, share with them about how your feeling about mentoring and ask for their prayer support. I'd also recommend praying with your spouse about your desires to mentor. If you are looking to mentor outside of your family, you might even want to include your children in this prayer journey.

Study the Scriptures

Being a biblical mentor requires being in the Word daily. Get yourself into this habit by using a Bible reading plan. If you fall behind, let the lost days go and simply pick up at the current day. God will be faithful to impress on your heart the Word, so give yourself the grace to not do it perfectly. I highly recommend checking out the IMMERSED Bible reading plan at *More to Be*. It's full of grace! In addition, I encourage you to find a Bible study to join in real life or online. Look for one that will help you grow personally as well as expand your understanding of the Scriptures.

Connect with Your Sisters in Christ

It is so important for you to connect with other believers in a way that will enable you to be nurtured, loved and encouraged. A Bible study, small prayer group, or an accountability group is an ideal way to do this, so make the commitment today. Find peers that will challenge and encourage you as you seek to become a woman of influence on the next generation. You will not only find kindred spirits through attending a Bible study or a Moms in Prayer (formerly Moms In Touch) group, but you might also find women who would be perfect ministry partners in forming a mentoring ministry group.

Be Accountable

As you move forward in this journey, be faithful in your church attendance and pray for the Lord to send women to mentor you.

In addition, if you are married, be sure to share with your husband your desire to mentor and as well as your commitment to grow spiritually. If he is not a believer, be patient with his limited understanding of your desires and pray for the right time to open your heart to him about why you want to mentor and how you see it playing out in your life.

Finally, it is so important to come under the authority of a spiritual leader, such as your pastor as well as the elders and/or leadership in your church. Go to your pastor and share your desire to impact women, including the next generation, through upholding the Titus 2 call. Relay to him what you've learned in this book and how you'd like to receive his support, guidance and leadership. Also seek your his perspective on your unique gifting and life circumstances, especially as it would pertain to serving the body of Christ in your own church and the world beyond.

Find

Look for Opportunities

Keep your eyes open and ready to notice the next generation eager for mentoring. If you're a mom, the Lord most certainly wants you to start with your children, so consider how you can intentionally mentor them starting today. Whether you have children, look beyond the walls of your home and into the community in which you live. Take notice of the tweens, teens, twenty-somethings, and women at your church, workplace, or neighborhood. Do some of them look lonely, discouraged, lost? Are they going through a difficult time? Could they use an extra word of encouragement or support? Do they seem teachable and eager to grow spiritually? The Lord may have in mind for you to begin a one-on-one mentoring relationship or to partner with another woman to begin an ETC group, host a Mugs & Mornings time, or lead a Grace Chats gathering (more about these opportunities in the following chapters).

Follow Through

Commit to the Call

Remember that you have been called by God to serve as a biblical mentor, not because you feel qualified but because you are qualified in Christ to be a woman of influence in the spreading of the Gospel. Make your commitment to the Lord and seek your approval from Him. Yes, you need to commit wholeheartedly to those you mentor, whether you are doing so in a one-on-one relationship or in a group setting. But your focus must be on the Lord, not on the people or the outcome. You do not want to be easily swayed by temperamental teens or emotionally driven women, so you must steady your focus and purpose on mentoring for the glory of God with an eternal perspective in mind. I would highly recommend spending time writing down one or two sentences why you are committing to the mentoring call, and posting it where your eyes can fall fresh on it regularly. You might even want to include a verse the drives you back to the truth as a clear reminder of your pure desire to be used as a mentor.

Don't Forget About Boundaries!

Nearly the most important aspect in having healthy relationships is having healthy boundaries, which we've discussed in detail already! But this point can't be emphasized enough. Be sure to set realistic goals for your time commitment, purpose, and desired outcome. Protect yourself from the trap of serving until you're burned out by putting healthy boundaries in place. If the idea of boundaries eludes you, please make the take time to read "Boundaries" by Cloud and Townsend before you begin your mentoring relationships, especially those outside your family unit.

Make the Most of More To Be

More to Be exists because the call to mentor is so misunderstood and the need is so great. This is why all the resources at www.moretobe.com are designed to equip women, like you, to embark on a mentoring journey, and yet are relevant for tweens, teens, twenty-somethings, and women of various ages and spiritual maturity. The *Topics & Truth* free downloads can be used for personal study, one-on-one conversation starters, or as handouts for an *ETC*, *Mugs & Mornings*, or *Grace Chat* gathering. The *Dig Deep Guides* enable you to go deeper personally or as a mentor, and are great to use as a leader of a mentoring group. You will also find all the necessary materials for beginning your own mentoring group plus an extensive collection of resources, so be sure to visit www.moretobe.com.

Take Time to Train

1. Now that you've read this "to do list," what steps are you ready to take first? Highlight them or jot them down in a notebook.
2. Next to those steps, indicate tentative dates in which you'd like to accomplish them as well as the name of someone who can hold you accountable.
3. Devote at least five minutes a day toward praying for those the Lord has positioned you to influence. Begin with your family, praying for each person by name, giving thanks to the Lord for their place in your life. Then continue on in your praying to lift up your friends, colleagues and acquaintances. Ask the Lord to reveal to you how to influence them for Christ. Finally, pray for those you feel God leading you to mentor.

~ • ~

CHAPTER TWENTY-FOUR

Impact Life

Biblical mentoring is a privilege, blessing and sanctification process. As we've learned throughout this journey, mentoring is about becoming a disciple of Christ, a doer of the Word, and a person who lives out her faith, one moment at a time.

Being a biblical mentor is also about pursuing intentional, authentic relationships with the next generation, in the context of faith. It is a response to the Titus 2 call to train up and make known the Word to the younger women, especially our daughters. It is a beautiful, God-ordained process that should be common place in our lives.

I challenge you to answer the call today to biblically mentor your daughters, nieces, friends, and neighbors, and any other women God brings into your life today.

Your basic training is complete, but the race is just beginning.

> *1 Corinthians 9:24-27 MSG*
> *You've all been to the stadium and seen the athletes race. Everyone runs; one wins. Run to win. All good athletes train hard. They do it for a gold medal that tarnishes and fades. You're after one that's gold eternally.*

I don't know about you, but I'm running hard for the finish line. I'm giving it everything I've got. No sloppy living for me! I'm staying alert and in top condition. I'm not going to get caught napping, telling everyone else all about it and then missing out myself.

May you choose this day to impact lives for the glory of God.

~ • ~

PART FIVE

Resources

She potentially missed out on watching a miracle because she was depending on herself to feed the people...It isn't me doing the work for God, but it is me trusting God to do the work in me...Worship, not work, flows out of the hearts of those who believe.

Emily P. Freeman
Grace for the Good Girl

Becoming a Disciple of Christ

You may not realize this truth, but the God of the Universe cares deeply for you. From the beginning of time, He has been calling out to His people to enter into a personal relationship with Him - a relationship built on the foundation of sacrificial love.

God is not merely some cosmic force, tossing the stars into the sky and spinning the earth into rotation, casually creating people and turning them loose like a wind up toy. God is Holy, perfect, intentional and purposeful. He is strong, powerful, tender, merciful and loving. He created us in His very image and longs for us to worship him wholeheartedly in everything we do.

As a part of His perfect plan, God desires for us to belong to the family of God as His beloved children. He is prepared to bestow on us this priceless gift of salvation and the richness of His inheritance, made possible only through faith in Jesus Christ as Lord and Savior.

> *Ephesians 1:3-13 ESV*
> *Blessed be the God and Father of our Lord Jesus Christ, who has blessed us in Christ with every spiritual blessing in the heavenly places, even as he chose us in him before the foundation of the world, that we should be holy and blameless before him. In love he predestined us for adoption as sons through Jesus Christ, according to the purpose of his will, to the praise of his glorious grace, with which he has blessed us in the Beloved. In him we have redemption through his blood, the forgiveness of our trespasses, according to the riches of his grace, which he lavished upon us, in all wisdom and insight making known to us the mystery of his will, according to his purpose, which he set forth in Christ as a plan for*

the fullness of time, to unite all things in him, things in heaven and things on earth.

In him we have obtained an inheritance, having been predestined according to the purpose of him who works all things according to the counsel of his will, so that we who were the first to hope in Christ might be to the praise of his glory. In him you also, when you heard the word of truth, the gospel of your salvation, and believed in him, were sealed with the promised Holy Spirit, who is the guarantee of our inheritance until we acquire possession of it, to the praise of his glory.

God is calling us into a relationship with Him through faith in His Son. The question is how will we respond to this call? Will we choose to ignore it, silence it, or let it go through to spiritual voicemail? Or will we respond to His call and embrace Jesus' sacrifice made on the cross on our behalf?

John 6:65 ESV
And he said, "This is why I told you that no one can come to me unless it is granted him by the Father."

Maybe the reason we hesitate is because we don't feel like we're good enough to hear from God? Maybe we're ashamed about our past mistakes? Maybe we're concerned that we'll never measure up to God's expectations?

It seems most of us can point out our imperfections rather quickly. We know what is wrong with us, even if we're wearing the mask of a perfectly poised woman in all of our social circles and churchy functions. The truth of the matter is that we'll never be able to get it all together and be good enough for God. We will always mess up. We will rebel against those in authority over us. Break promises. Betray friends. Burden our lives with thoughts and actions we know are wrong. We're a mess, plain and simple. That's because we are sinners.

2 Corinthians 5:20-21 ESV
Therefore, we are ambassadors for Christ, God making his appeal through us. We implore you on behalf of Christ, be reconciled to

God. For our sake he made him to be sin who knew no sin, so that in him we might become the righteousness of God.

Sin is disobedience against God's will, as revealed through His Word and the working of the Holy Spirit. The Scriptures are full of wonderful instructions on how to live, what to watch out for, what to steer clear from and how to treat others. But in our desire to be in control (and be our own god), we dismiss God's instruction and head down our own course of destruction. This disobedience erects a wall between us and God, and it also damages our earthly relationships. As we live with pride, bitterness, betrayal, lack of forgiveness, deception, and so on, we grow further and further away from those we love and especially God.

Ephesians 2:8-9
God saved you by his grace when you believed. And you can't take credit for this; it is a gift from God.
Salvation is not a reward for the good things we have done, so none of us can boast about it.

It may seem utterly incomprehensible, but our merciful, creator God has allowed His Son, Jesus Christ, to make a way to tear down those walls erected by our sin and open the gates to eternity. When Jesus took the punishment for our sin on the cross, His shed blood became the wrecking ball that knocks down the wall between us and God. He came to the earth because of God's perfect plan to rescue His people. He died on the cross, shedding His blood as the only necessary (atoning) sacrifice for our sin. When He rose from the grave, He proved that God's Word was true and that the sacrifice of His death was totally acceptable before God.

As we walk this earth, we will feel the consequences of our sin in our human condition, but we no longer have to live in that mess apart from God. We also have the hope of eternal life, promised only to those who believe in Jesus Christ as Lord.

John 3:16 ESV
For God so loved the world, that he gave his only Son, that

whoever believes in him should not perish but have eternal life.

Even though it wasn't His fault, Jesus Christ took upon Himself the burden of our sin because of His love for His Father demonstrated by His obedience to the point of death. So what is expected in return? Simply put, God wants us to tell Him about our sin and our need for a Savior (confession), as we turn from our wrong-doing into right living (repentance). He wants us to receive His forgiveness, grace and mercy as a sign of His love. Most of all, He wants us to live for His glory, and not our own, as He offers us a peace and joy that we have never experienced before.

Romans 10:9-10
If you confess with your mouth that Jesus is Lord and believe in your heart that God raised him from the dead, you will be saved. For it is by believing in your heart that you are made right with God, and it is by confessing with your mouth that you are saved.

When we surrender our lives to Christ, He not only tears down the wall between us and God, but He also gives us the Holy Spirit to become our personal guide. He also paves the road to heaven with an overflowing measure of hope, grace, love, mercy and forgiveness, showing us how to live as sinners saved by grace.

2 Corinthians 5:17
This means that anyone who belongs to Christ has become a new person. The old life is gone; a new life has begun!

God knows we will never be able to make ourselves good enough to be in a relationship with Him, so He gives us Christ to make us right and change us from the inside out. In doing so, He also changes us from the outside in, making us a living testimony for others to witness the power of God at work in a sinner's life. In Christ, we become a new creation who can live with an eternal perspective -- a perspective that brings life, hope and purpose into sharp focus as we discover God's unfolding plan. Don't you think that is a better way to live?

Would you like to experience life transformed today?

Apart from faith in Christ as Lord and Savior, our earthly experience is lived without a personal relationship with God, and the outcome is dire. Even in our death, we will not see the promises of heaven, unless we have believed that Jesus is indeed the Risen King. I encourage you to take a step of faith and invite Jesus into your life as your Redeemer by praying something similar to this:

> *God, I believe that you are good, right, holy, and true. Even though I may not understand everything about you or the Bible, I can admit that I know that I am a sinner, who has messed up before and will continue to make mistakes in the future. I am not perfect, but You are always perfect. I am not good enough by my standard, but that is not your standard. You're not looking for my goodness. You're looking for my love. I want to love you God. Will you show me how? Thank you, God, for sending Your Son, Jesus Christ, to die for my sins and make me right with you. I believe that His sacrifice on the cross paid the price for all my sin. Thank you for your forgiveness. Thank you that I don't have to earn your love, but that You give it to me as a gift. Please come into my life as my Lord and Savior. I give you my life, my heart, my all. I want to live for You from now on. I surrender my life to You. In Jesus' Strong Name, Amen.*

If you asked Jesus to come into your life as Lord, then it is my deepest joy to welcome to the family of God, sister.

Now it is time for you to live your life as a true disciple of Christ.

God is delighted to be in charge of your life. He never takes us by force, but He will give us His power when we ask for it. Start today, speaking with God as you would a friend, about the areas in your life that are a mess. Ask Him to show you how to live right. Ask Him to show you His purposes for you and how to invest in this world with an eternal perspective. Wait, expectantly, to see what He'll accomplish in you as you yield every thought and action to Him.

Grab a Bible and start reading the book of John. Ask the Lord to provide a mentor to help you along your brand new journey of becoming the woman God intended. And be sure to seek out a local church that teaches the Word of God as truth. Make an appointment to speak with the pastor and share with him how you've begun a new life as a disciple of Christ.

Scripture References
John 6:44,65; Ephesians 2:8-10; Romans 10:9; Matthew 10:32-33; 1 John 1:9; Acts 2:38; Acts 3:1; 2 Corinthians 5:21-22; Romans 5:1; Romans 4:16; Romans 1:16-17; Romans 10:9-13; Romans 8:5-11; Romans 2:4-5; Romans 6:1-8; Romans 12:1-2; 2 Corinthians 5:17

~ • ~

Recommended Resources

As you embark on your mentoring journey, I highly recommend these resources to help you launch forward into biblical mentoring, passionate about impacting the next generation.

Books

- NIV/The Message Parallel Bible, Personal Size
- *Disciplines Of The Beautiful Woman*, Anne Ortlund
- *Lord, Teach Me to Pray in 28 Days*, Kay Arthur
- *Discerning the Voice of God: How to Recognize When God Speaks*, Priscilla Shirer
- *Grace for the Good Girl: Letting Go of the Try-Hard Life*, Emily P. Freeman
- *Spiritual Mothering: The Titus 2 Model for Women Mentoring Women*, Susan Hunt
- *Leading Women to the Heart of God*, Lysa TerKeurst
- *Boundaries,* Dr. Henry Cloud and Dr. John Townsend
- *A Woman's Guide to Servant Leadership: A Biblical Study of Becoming a Christlike Leader*, Rhonda H. Kelley
- *Breaking Free,* Beth Moore
- *Praying God's Word*, Beth Moore
- *Get Out of That Pit*, Beth Moore
- *The Five Love Languages of Teenagers*, Gary Chapman
- *From the Trash Pile to the Treasure Chest: Creating a Godly Legacy*, Leah Adams

Websites

- Focus on the Family ~ http://www.focusonthefamily.com/
- Family Life ~ http://www.familylife.com/
- MODSquad, Mothers of Daughters ~ http://modsquadblog.com/
- inCourage ~ http://www.incourage.me/
- Moms in Prayer International ~ http://www.momsintouch.org/
- Internet Cafe Devotions ~ http://internetcafedevotions.com/
- The Rebelution ~ http://www.therebelution.com/
- Pam Stenzel ~ http://www.pamstenzel.com/
- True Woman ~ http://www.truewoman.com/
- Top Trends of 2011: Millennials Rethink Christianity ~ http://www.barna.org
- Mom Heart Online ~ http://www.momheart.org/
- Women Living Well ~ http://www.womenlivingwell.org
- The Better Mom ~ http://www.thebettermom.com
- Good Morning Girls ~ http://www.goodmorninggirls.org/
- Hello Mornings ~ http://inspiredtoaction.com/hellomornings/register/

Especially at More to Be

- **Topics & Truth FREE Downloads** ~ http://www.moretobe.com/downloads/
- Topics: dating, relationships, conflict, prayer, time management, getting real with God, studying Scripture, identity, worth, mental makeover, beauty, spiritual gifts and personality traits
- **ETC Mentoring, Mugs & Mornings, Grace Chats** ~ http://www.moretobe.com/etc/
  Information: detailed instruction for forming an ETC or Mugs & Mornings mentoring group as well as hosting Grace Chats, including invitation options, checklists, and training manual
- **Life Coaching** ~ http://www.moretobe.com/life-coaching/
  Services: life coaching opportunities are available for moms and mentors as well as women in leadership roles

*Please keep in mind that while I recommend the books and websites listed above, the views of the authors, writers, and organizations will not always reflect my personal or theological beliefs nor be consistent with the overall message shared here. If you come across questionable content, please do let me know. I also highly recommend seeking counsel from your pastor regarding spiritual matters.

~ • ~

Small Group Leader's Guide

Proverbs 11:25
...those who refresh others will themselves be refreshed.

If I could see you face to face, I would be beaming with a smile, clapping my hands together and offering you the most sincere encouraging words for even considering leading a small group through *Impact My Life*. I know this is no small task for you. Likely you are a leader by God's design and He has birthed in you a passion for not only the next generation but a desire to see women equipped with the Word.

Whether you are considering using *Impact My Life* with your women's ministry team, a group of moms, an online Bible study discussion, or with potential ETC, Mugs & Mornings, or Grace Chat ministry leaders, let me encourage you to step out in faith. However, let me also urge you to seek the covering of prayer and Godly counsel. We women can overcommit and end up burnt out, brittle, and bitter. I do not want that for you. But I do want you to receive the blessing of teaching God's Word and imparting His Truth for His glory.

Suggested Guidelines

As you consider hosting and leading a small group, keep in mind the following guidelines, which are merely suggestions, but will enable you to facilitate a positive experience for yourself as a leader and cultivate healthy relationships within your group.

Prayer

Devote a considerable amount of time to prayer regarding leading a small group before you even make decision about doing so. Once you have peace to move forward, continue to pray about who to invite. Throughout the five weeks of studying *Impact My Life*, dedicate time to praying for each one of the participants. Be sure to open and close each gathering with prayer, seeking the participation of others in this prayer time. Also, find a good Christian friend or an older godly women to pray for you in your role as leader.

Listen & Learn

The temptation as a leader is to fix a participant's problems. Only Jesus, however, can truly change a life, and He does so through the working of the Holy Spirit. Strive to listen carefully to your participants with a desire to learn about them so that you can pray specifically for them. Ask the Holy Spirit to lead and guide your every word, so that when you do respond, you can be confident you are doing so by His grace and for His purpose.

Encourage with Humility

The best thing you can do as a leader is to be in the trenches with the group. Be willing to be vulnerable, with discretion, on areas of struggle and challenge. And at the same time, consider each word you contribute with the filter, "Is this beneficial?" Guard against sharing simply to fill the silence. Let the pause of questions and reflections be a time for God to quicken a person's heart and impart a Truth.

Keep It Confidential

From the very beginning, set the policy forth that everything shared within the group remains in the group. I recommend using the expression, "If it is not our story, personally, then it is not our story to tell." I would highly recommend opening or closing each session with this reminder.

Suggested Format

I recommend six weeks dedicated to moving through *Impact My Life* with a small group. This will allow for a sweet, unhurried introduction session and a meaningful closing fellowship time. I also would suggest an hour and a half session. Be sure to begin promptly and end on time, as everyone's time is sacred, including yours. If you feel the momentum of conversation, pause for a moment to let those who must go leave and press on for another 15 minutes to wrap up. Also, keep the set up and clean up simple. Have a tea basket on hand, coffee and water, but feel free to pass on something to eat. Most of us don't need it anyhow!

The following structure is designed for using the book alone for a small group study. If your group would like to go deeper, you can also get the *Impact My Life Study Guide*, which is a companion resource and lays out a more in-depth study course.

Week 1

Introduction and Get to Know Each Other

Allow time for each woman to introduce herself, share her faith story and/or mentoring story, and explain why she'd like to learn more about mentoring.

Week 2

Part 1: Mentoring Simplified

{Chapters 1 through 4}
Work through Part 1 of *Impact My Life*, highlighting different aspects of each chapter, studying the Scripture verses together, confessing your individual excuses, and discussing the Take Time to Train questions.

Week 3

Part 2: Eliminating Excuses

{Chapters 5 through 11}
Move through Part 2 with a desire to dig into the nitty gritty of mentoring. Share ideas of how to mentor practically, personally, and purposefully. Also take time to look closely at the Scripture verses and discuss the Take Time to Train questions.

Week 4

Part 3: M.E.N.T.O.R.I.N.G.

{Chapters 12 through 21}
During this portion of the study, continue to focus on rounding out your understanding of mentoring through looking closely at the Scripture passages, answering the Take Time to Train questions and allowing for time to share about your experiences with mentoring as well as any concerns about mentoring int the future.

Week 5

Part 4: Impact My Life

{Chapters 22 through 24}
As you move into Part 4, devote time to praying about the opportunities to begin mentoring one-on-one or more formally using the ETC mentoring model. See if any of the women in your group desire to lead a mentoring group and begin discussing the

process of how this might become reality. Also make time to study the Scripture verses and discuss the Take Time to Train questions.

Week 6

Gather for Prayer and Fellowship

This meeting time is designed for the sake of fellowship, praise, and prayer. Plan a potluck brunch, lunch, or evening desert time to enjoy one another. Share what you've learned, how you've been challenged, and what you feel God is leading you to do as a mentor. Devote a good portion to a time of praise and prayer!

Thank you so much for your willingness to host a small group discussion of *Impact My Life*. It is truly a blessing and honor to know that God will use this material to impact the lives of the women you are leading and the precious ones that will be influenced by them.

As a way of thanking you for leading, you can request a special discount of 15% off a life coaching package of your choosing. To learn more, about the benefits of life coaching, email me directly at elisa@elisapulliam.com.

~ • ~

Forming a Mentoring Group

As we've been discussing throughout *Impact My Life*, the opportunity to mentor can occur in one-on-one relationships or in a group setting. While the group mentoring idea may be new to you, it is a tested method that provides a beautiful setting for impacting lives.

The group mentoring method can be used with tweens, teens, twenty-somethings, or women, especially moms. Your desire to lead a particular group will certainly reflect your passion, calling, and circumstances.

etc

evening tea and chat

creating a place for tweens, teens, and twenty-somethngs to get real answers to their real questions

Mentoring groups can be as small as three participants. Size doesn't matter. If the Lord grows your group to beyond fifteen, you may opt to break into small groups. Your gathering can be hosted at a home, school, or church, depending on the setting that works best for you and your participants.

As you consider hosting a mentoring group, you have a choice for what you'd like to call it. ETC, which stands for Evening Tea & Chat, is meant for an evening time slot, while Mugs & Mornings is designed for a morning meeting time. It really comes down to deciding what is better for your schedule and that of your participants. Regardless of the name, the purpose and format is the same. We also have Grace Chats, which is designed especially for moms of tweens and teens, which you can read about below.

Hosting & Leading

Hosting and leading a mentoring group is simple:

Partnership

Find at least one Christian woman to partner with you in hosting and leading your ministry. A group of two or three is ideal, but not necessary.

Location

Pick a location, such as a home, church or school, for your gatherings.

Date & Time

Set a bimonthly date with a 2-hour commitment.

Invite Girls

Invite Christian and non-Christian tweens, teens, or twenty-somethings from church, your community, or amongst your daughter's friends. Ideally, a group should consider age span, such as 10-13, 14-18, 19-22, 23-26, 26 and beyond, moms of tweens, moms of teens, etc.

Tea

Provide lots of hot water and a collection of tea bags, or hot chocolate, for the girls to grab upon their arrival. Remember, fill your tea basket!

Index Cards

Also have on hand a stack of index cards, pens and a small basket.

Topics & Truth

Pick a Topics & Truth free download to print out for yourself and the group. Work through the topic in about 10-15 minutes, teaching the main points. You may also purchase the Dig Deep Guides, which are full of illustration ideas, questions and tips.

Q&A Time

While the topic is being taught, invite your group to write down questions -- about anything -- on index cards and toss them in a basket. Working with your partner, for the next forty minutes, take turns answering their questions with a Scripture reference in the context of life application. Feel free to use a personal example, but remember that less is often more! If you don't know an answer, skip that question with a mention to follow up one-on-one.

Prayer

Close the time in prayer, then encourage the group to get a second cup of tea.

Authentic Relationships

While the group is relaxing and sipping tea, be available for one-on-one conversations. Let the relationships grow naturally.

WHAT ABOUT OFFERING GRACE CHATS FOR MOMS?

Hosting a mentoring group is an awesome way to impact the next generation. Whether you choose to do ETC or Mugs & Morning, your impact will be palpable. If your group is designed for tweens and teens, it can also open the door to providing a time for their moms.

Grace CHATS
creating a place for moms
to connect and be inspired

If you can find women to partner with you, we highly recommend offering Grace Chats for their mothers. It isn't only the next generation that needs encouragement! Many mothers are at a loss for how to deal with the issues facing their daughters. By hosting Grace Chats, which uses the same format as ETC or Mugs & Mornings, older women can step into significant mentoring relationships with younger moms. To learn more about forming a Grace Chats mentoring group, email more@moretobe.com.

I hope you'll prayerfully consider beginning a mentoring ministry using our group mentoring format. If you have any questions, please email more@moretobe.com or visit www.moretobe.com for further information and resources.

~ • ~

About More to Be

2 Corinthians 3:16-18 MSG
...when God is personally present, a living Spirit... Nothing between us and God, our faces shining with the brightness of his face. And so we are transfigured much like the Messiah, our lives gradually becoming brighter and more beautiful as God enters our lives and we become like him.

More to Be is dedicated to engaging the next generation through equipping moms of tweens and teens with biblically relevant resources and encouraging women to step into significant mentoring roles.

As a ministry, we believe that God designed us to be a multigenerational people, where the older generation of women should be involved and invested in training up the young women in their lives (Titus 2:3-5). Because of this belief, *More to Be* is committed to equipping Christian women with resources packed with practical mentoring principles and life application ideas. These resources include the ETC, Mugs & Mornings, and Grace Chats mentoring programs, Topics & Truth free downloads, in-depth Dig Deep Guides and opportunities for life coaching.

At the heart of *More to Be* is a vision to see women (young and old) become more bright, more beautiful, more like Jesus as a personally relevant God enters their lives (2 Corinthians 3:16-18 MSG) through mentoring relationships and resources steeped in biblical truth. This is what it means to experience life transformed -- a life where there is more to be as we become more like Him and impact the world around us.

If you have any questions about *More to Be*, please email more@moretobe.com or visit www.moretobe.com. If you'd like to learn more about life coaching, please visit www.elisapulliam.com or email elisa@elisapulliam.com.

~ • ~

About the Author

Ephesians 3:7
By God's grace and mighty power, I have been given the privilege of serving him by spreading this Good News.

Elisa Pulliam, who prefers to be called Lisa, is a lifelong mentor, ministry leader, speaker and life coach, passionate about encouraging and equipping this generation of women to impact the next generation with relevant Truth.

After more than a decade of mothering and over seventeen years of mentoring teen girls coinciding with leading women's ministries, Elisa is in tune with the struggles of teens, twenty-somethings and today's women. Having lived a life apart from God, marked by a legacy of dysfunction and a long season of rebellion, Elisa understands the power of the Cross. When she met Jesus as her Lord and Savior during her junior year in college, her life radically changed, and her life calling soon emerged.

Elisa's deepest desire is to facilitate life transformation in others by offering practical, easily accessible and biblically sound resources to touch the heart, mind and soul. She shares her insights, teaching materials, and mentoring resources at *More to B*e, and offers life coaching through elisapulliam.com. You can also find her contributing monthly Mothers of Daughters.com and The Better Mom.com.

When the Lord provides the opportunity, Elisa thoroughly enjoys speaking at women's events and for groups of teenagers, especially at Redefining Beauty Events. She connects with her audience through storytelling as she shares her personal experiences in the context of biblical truth. Teens, twenty-somethings, and Christian women respond to her messages, because she is transparent and doesn't hold back from tossing in a good bit of humor as she unravels life lessons.

Elisa's counts it pure joy to be Stephen's wife, who is not only her best friend but has been Christ-with-skin-on to her for more than 17 years of marriage. She also considers it a privilege to train up her four children (ages 8 through 14), and admits that they have taught her the most about love, affection and total forgiveness.

~ • ~

Acknowledgements

1 Corinthians 10:31
...do it all for the glory of God.

My experience as a mentor, and my ability to capture it in this book, would never be possible without the incredible support of my pit crew. As Michael Hyatt refers to in hist book, Platform, everyone needs a group of people who make it possible to do what you feel called to do, in the same way a race car driver needs his pit crew to keep his car running.

I give thanks and so much honor to my husband, Stephen, who not only has been Christ with skin on to me for more than 16 years of marriage, but has also served as my unofficial life coach. Bless his heart, for listening to more than his fill of word quota, for more hours than any human should ever have to endure. Because of his support, I am able to have those couch conversations with teens, lead the ministry of *More to Be*, and delight in the calling of being a life coach.

It is a sweet blessing to also thank my children for their demonstration of grace as I invest in lives beyond the walls of our home. Their patience afforded me many writing hours as well! In particular, my two older daughters devoted time to proofreading and reviewing the content and design, which is both an opportunity I am delighted to offer them and a gift I am blessed to receive.

As I think of how this book took shape, I am keenly aware of how our two babysitters demonstrated for me the art of mentoring and spurred me on to want to give this gift to others. Brannon and Natalie,

I love you both more than words could ever explain. You are like my own daughters, forever and always. Thank you for the way you love our family, join me in work of *More to Be*, and remind me of God's faithfulness.

I would also be remiss if I did not mention the role my extended family has played in this project through the many, many hours they've sacrificed, enabling my husband and I to continue serve our school community and engage with teens in creative and practical ways. These opportunities opened my eyes to the needs of this generation and fueled my passion to make biblical mentoring simple for you. Mom, Andrea, and Nana, thank you!

To be honest, this book would likely not exist if it wasn't for Trina Holden. Her thought-provoking post at the Allume blog inspired me to step out in faith in forming a mastermind group, Brew1024. Around the same time, Trina also personally encouraged me to take the 31 Days of Mentoring eBook to the next level and to use my mastermind group for feedback. I needed a cheerleader with the voice of a coach, and God delivered, first Trina and then my Brewsistahs! Thank you ladies for the role each played in this project.

My pit crew would not be complete without the amazing women who serve on the More to Be team along with a core group of friends who keep me grounded and motivated. In the midst of their busy lives and unique callings, they somehow find the time to offer feedback, encouragement and accountability. A special thanks to Kathy, Linda and Lea for their sacrifice of time in proofreading. Any mistake found within is due entirely to my last minute changes, and not their editing expertise.

I am also incredibly grateful for the Impact My Life Launch Team and the way they were used by the Lord to provide support, encouragement and prayer. May you go forth as women of Impact!

A special word of thanks is in store for Travis Peterson, a pastor with a heart for the Lord and a desire to see women rise up to places of influence in line with the Titus 2 call. He stepped in at a most critical time to offer his feedback on the manuscript. His words of wisdom brought great insights and sharpened the message significantly. Pastor Travis, thank you for shepherding this part of the flock hundreds of miles away, and for offering your teaching in such a humble and caring manner.

Of course, anything that comes from my hands is all for the glory of God and a result of the work of my Lord and Savior, Jesus Christ. Without His obedience to the Father, where would any of us be? I'm sure that without Jesus, there would be no way I'd be living this life impacting the next generation and inspiring you to do the same. Thank you Jesus for this life and this work.

To God be the glory.

~ • ~

Praise for Impact My Life

"*Impact My Life* is a beautiful call to women everywhere to step up to the plate, take the initiative and pour your life into the next generation. Elisa gives you a step by step guide on how to be a Biblical mentor while also inspiring courage and a vision. This is an excellent book filled with guidance and resources that I highly recommend!"

Courtney Joseph
~ Women Living Well

"Women by God's design crave relationship. In a world of instant tweets and social media, it seems that the ministry of mentoring and discipling have taken a seat in the back row of many churches, leaving our women and girls hungry for deeper, authentic relationships.
In Elisa Pulliam's new book, *Impact My Life*: Biblical Mentoring Simplified, she gives women of every age, denomination and background the essential tools and encouragement they need to pursue the passion of Jesus' heart to be in meaningful discipleship relationships with each other.

Elisa lays out practically what Biblical mentoring should look like and the way to make that happen. She encourages the reader with chapters such as "I Lack Wisdom and I'm Too Young," while breaking down the ministry of mentoring with a brilliant acronym of M.E.N.T.O.R.I.N.G. It's these creative, practical, Biblical tools that remind each reader that she is qualified to mentor and to invest into the kingdom through relationship with other women. The excuses stop here. In a world of constant communication, this is just the tool that can lead women into deeper, discipling connections with the women in their sphere of influence. It's certainly one that I will be using as

I lead a group of women through a year long season of intentional discipleship. This book is a blessing!"

Lori Macmath
~ Co-Owner of Internet Cafe Devotions

"In *Impact My Life*, Lisa Pulliam takes you step by step how to grow your ministry as a mentor. This is valuable resource for anyone who shares her passion to develop women in their relationship with Christ. Lisa quite simply has the heart of a mentor and her desire is to share all that she has learned with you as well. I know you will be blessed by her encouragement."

Stacey Thacker
~ Mothers of Daughters &
Co-Author Hope for the Weary Mom

"As someone with a growing passion for mentoring, Lisa's handbook for having an impact is timely and practical. The content is well organized and easy to dip in to depending on where you are in your mentoring journey. Not sure you're mentor material? She'll convince you otherwise. Don't know where to start? She lists dozens of materials and conversation starters. Want to know what it looks like to mentor? She paints an exciting and motivating picture what it looks like to change lives through mentoring. This book will impact you as it motivates and equips you to pursue purposeful, authentic relationships with the women around you."

Trina Holden
~ All That Is Good

"Mentoring simplified! Elisa Pulliam's *Impact My Life* ebook on the ins and outs of mentoring is a treasure chest of wisdom on the topic of mentoring. While mentoring is not rocket science, neither is it something that should be entered into lightly or without significant time spent in prayer. Everyone has a story....a story that can help someone else on their journey through life. *Impact My Life* encourages women in the authentic sharing of their life and story with a younger-in-the-faith woman or girl to help them on their own journey of faith. Short chapters, abundant use of Scripture and frequent prompts to ponder the topic of discussion all combine to make *Impact My Life* a book that every woman who is serious about leaving a lasting legacy and impacting future generations should read."

Leah Adams
~ The Point Ministries

"In *Impact My Life*, Elisa reminds us that mentoring is a type of modern day discipleship that Jesus began by modeling His faith in His actions, such as when He took the time out to listen and answer each of His disciples questions, responded to their daily needs and challenged them in their call to glorify God. Every day we can follow Jesus' steps in our daily lives where ever we are: at work, in our homes, in our church or even at the mall! Mentoring is a form of discipleship designed to impart biblical truth and bring that truth into life through teaching, correcting, modeling and encouraging in a committed, accountable relationship. You may still feel hesitant about the call to mentor but as you read this book, you'll find that everyday as you live out your Christian walk, you are mentoring to those God has brought into your life as you shine Christ's light and share your life with them."

Samantha
~ Mom & Mentor

~ • ~

Have you been impacted?

I'd love to hear from you!

elisa@elisapulliam.com

https://twitter.com/elisapulliam

http://www.elisapulliam.com

Spread the Word!

http://www.moretobe.com

http://www.facebook.com/moretobe

http://www.twitter.com/moretobe

http://www.pinterest.com/elisapulliam

Made in the USA
San Bernardino, CA
11 April 2014